Zion Earth Zen Sky is full of nourishing wisdom. Charles Inouye constantly uses the ideas of Buddhism, Japanese culture, and other literary and philosophical ideas he has dealt with in his academic work to illuminate ideas about how to deal with living in a fallen world full of suffering. His ideas, while sometimes unorthodox, are fully consistent with Latter-day Saint scripture and prophetic counsel. I have never read a better book showing how Buddhist principles can illuminate and enrich our understanding of the gospel.

—Andrew Hall
Associate Professor of Modern East Asian
History, Kyushu University, Fukuoka, Japan

Each life is unique. But perhaps some lives are more unique than others. As readers are guided along Charles Inouye's life journey, they may be surprised at how different his experiences are from theirs. (Fortunately, there's a glossary at the back to help us with the unique language of his life.) And yet, his warmth and candor eventually draw us into his inimitable world, and we become friends who enjoy a common vocabulary, a shared poetic sense, and a mutual spiritual understanding. The result is that we, with Charles, can understand and savor an otherwise inscrutable haiku like this:

almost late for class—
I cry for Henry and for
Akutagawa

—Jack Stoneman
Associate Professor of Japanese,
Brigham Young University

A
Living Faith
Book

Living Faith books are for readers who cherish the life of the mind and the things of the Spirit. Each title is a unique example of faith in search of understanding, the voice of a scholar who has cultivated a believing heart while engaged in the disciplines of the Academy.

Other Living Faith books include:

Adam S. Miller, *Letters to a Young Mormon* (2nd ed.)

Samuel M. Brown, *First Principles and Ordinances: The Fourth Article of Faith in Light of the Temple*

Steven L. Peck, *Evolving Faith: Wanderings of a Mormon Biologist*

Patrick Q. Mason, *Planted: Belief and Belonging in an Age of Doubt*

Ashley Mae Hoiland, *One Hundred Birds Taught Me to Fly: The Art of Seeking God*

Thomas F. Rogers, *Let Your Hearts and Minds Expand: Reflections on Faith, Reason, Charity, and Beauty*

George B. Handley, *If Truth Were a Child: Essays*

Melissa Wei-Tsing Inouye, *Crossings: A Bald Asian American Latter-day Saint Woman Scholar's Ventures through Life, Death, Cancer, & Motherhood (Not Necessarily in That Order)*

George B. Handley, *The Hope of Nature: Our Care for God's Creations*

James E. Faulconer, *Thinking Otherwise: Theological Explorations of Joseph Smith's Revelations*

Samuel M. Brown, *Where the Soul Hungers: One Doctor's Journey from Atheism to Faith*

zion

earth

zen

sky

Zion Earth Zen Sky

a memoir by CHARLES SHIRŌ INOUYE

A
Living Faith
Book

BYU
Maxwell
Institute

The paper used in this publication meets the minimum requirements of the American National Standard for Information Sciences—Permanence of Paper for Printed Library Materials. ANSI Z39.48-19.

ISBN: 978-1-9503-0411-0

Art direction: Blair Hodges
Cover design: Heather Ward
Book design: Carmen Durland Cole

http://maxwellinstitute.byu.edu

Library of Congress Cataloging-in-Publication Data

Names: Inouye, Charles Shirō, author.
Title: Zion earth zen sky / by Charles Shirō Inouye.
Other titles: Living faith book (Neal A. Maxwell Institute for Religious Scholarship)
Description: Provo, UT : BYU Maxwell Institute, [2021] | Series: A living faith book | Summary: "Zion Earth Zen Sky is a candid account of both spiritual failure and success, written by a flawed yet hopeful person for the benefit of imperfect people"—Provided by publisher.
Identifiers: LCCN 2021005677 | ISBN 9781950304110 (paperback)
Subjects: LCSH: Inouye, Charles Shirō. | Mormons—Biography. | Japanese Americans—Biography. | LCGFT: Autobiographies.
Classification: LCC BX8695.I55 A3 2021 | DDC 289.3092 [B]—dc23
LC record available at https://lccn.loc.gov/2021005677

Printed in the United States of America by Sheridan Books, Inc.

To Mie, Leif, Kan, Satsuki, and Hank

The gods once were as we are now, and someday we will be like them. So let us put our speculations away, and write about the moments we walked together—when we cried in sorrow, and when we had hope.

IO FUI GIA' QUEL CHE VOI SIETE
E QUEL CHI SON
VOI ANCOR SARETE

I was once what you are now,
And as I am
You will be.

—From "The Holy Trinity" by Masaccio

And the Lord called his people Zion, because they were of one heart and one mind, and dwelt in righteousness; and there was no poor among them.

—Moses 7:18

There is a Japanese saying, "Fall down seven times, get up eight." *Nana korobi, ya oki.* But shouldn't it be, "Fall down seven times, get up seven?" How can you get up eight times if you only fall seven? Or is the idea that you have to get up the first time in order to fall the first time?

Contents

Foreword

I HAVE ALWAYS ADMIRED CHARLES INOUYE. I HAVE BEEN FOL-
lowing him around one way or another, like a pesky kid brother, for
the past four decades. As our professional and personal paths have
crossed, our sporadic but wide-ranging conversations—which
have covered matters as diverse as Japanese literature, faith, fly fishing, and memory—have always left me with new ways to see the
world. This book gives you, the reader, a chance to experience that
same invitation to widen your perspective on a range of topics, to
see the world in new ways. It is a gift from someone who hum-
bly describes himself as a "farm boy" but also portrays thinking as
"exercise" and whose creative prose and poetry combine to take
readers on a journey that follows one life but seemingly encom-
passes the cosmos.

Readers cannot be faulted for approaching this work initially as
a first-person *Bildungsroman*, that quintessential Western novel-
like genre that invites us to focus on a main character and follow
along the circuitous path of their youth and adulthood, watching
their development (*Bildung*) happen in a logical, if still entertaining

and often suspenseful, course. And Charles's chronological form and first-person voice, especially in its sincere and self-deprecating tone, ascribes to conventions of that genre. In a way, the autobiographical mode is the story's ground, its *Zion earth*.

However, the *haiku* poetry interspersed throughout the work, the seemingly random changes of focus, and the nonlinear nature of the narrative may at first seem out of place, even jarring to readers expecting either an autobiography or a novel. Yet that *jarring* is precisely the point of Charles's choice to write in the manner he does, effecting the kind of shock to the rational mind that is invoked by the Zen practice of using unanswerable riddles, *kōan*, to disrupt logical expectations and invite questions about where the tale, or life, is going. Such a multigeneric, roving point of view is the story's atmosphere, its *Zen sky*.

I mentioned that the work looks very much like a novel; I should also note that it is often very similar to Japanese *haibun*, a combination of short verse (*haiku*) and narrative (*bun*) that derives its literary cachet from brief narrative descriptions setting the scene for the short-form poetry that follows. Its sparse mode is the antithesis of encyclopedic nineteenth-century Anglo-American novelists, with a teasing ambiguity of empty space inviting the imagination to fill in the details. In *haibun* we witness a kind of twofold aesthetic approach to narrative that, like postmodernism, offers an alternative to the dominant Western mode of authorial, highly descriptive storytelling. Instead, *haibun* offers both writer and reader two complementary, and often asymmetrical, modes of expression. The narrative may be seen to set the stage, to establish context for the following verse(s), or it may carry a kind of aesthetic weight of its own. Likewise, the *haiku* may be cryptic distillations of the narrated experience, a kind of mnemonic retelling or lyrical "amen!" to the narrative. Or, as Charles notes toward the end of the book, *haiku* may help us cultivate the "ability to feel the power of the world directly." His verse may serve to point us in a direction far beyond simple description: a tumble from a tractor leading to stitches in the hospital can encapsulate the whole of growing up; a flowering weed against the moonlight can represent the essence of spiritual community.

His story is simultaneously old and new. As the child of Japanese American internment victims, he finds himself growing up in the rural Intermountain West as both outsider and insider, echoing the tension and discovery found in legions of second-generation immigrant American stories. Yet he brings a unique spin to the usual tale of finding one's place in a new world: his proximity to and eventual lifelong affiliation with a faith that is evangelically multiethnic and self-consciously syncretic but also aspires to peculiarity and homogeneity. His story describes his interaction with this curious faith—containing "the imaginative genius of Joseph Smith and the organizational brilliance of his successor . . . both still alive and in full tension with each other"—to which he converts and then reconverts over and over again. His continued exercise of faith helps him transcend the frontier ethos of his boyhood town and brings profound human insights to his interactions with marginalized Paiutes as well as pairings with spiritual principles from Buddhism.

His evocation of the metaphor of "raking," a physical task shared by high desert farmers and Zen practitioners alike, transforms the nature of this conversion narrative, a genre often dependent upon sudden, grandiose epiphanies, into a tale that underscores the role simple, ongoing, and necessary acts of devotion—raking—play in the spiritual quest for both enlightenment and transcendence. "There is no such thing as perfection. There is only raking." The task is not one we would naturally choose to do but one that is assigned to us, and we are bound to it. The rewards may seem slim—especially because the world interferes, and we are constantly needing to rerake. But, as Charles eloquently describes, "learning to extend yourself to someone else is the essence of the gospel. Indeed, it is the essence of human existence. It is nothing less than our reason for being." By and by we learn, as he does, that our raking is not *for* God but rather a means of helping us learn to rake *with* God: "Of all the things we can experience in this world, nothing compares to the feeling of helping others receive God's love." By emphasizing the quotidian nature of his personal faith journey, he models transcending the local to achieve a global, even divine, vision, fueled by a quest for self-knowledge and a desire to love others without judgment.

I find numerous admirable and compelling things about this work. First is its honesty. In an age of irony, the absence of guile in the narrative voice reminds me of Montaigne at his finest, although absent the latter's robust essaying forward. Charles's style is more after the medieval Japanese manner of *zuihitsu*, a narrative essay form invoking the meandering sense of going wherever one's brush seems to be leading. Second is its lyrical, even elegiac, descriptions of life in a world where accidents and unexpected events can suddenly flood out fields and farms, leaving "fish glistening on the roads." He has an evocative gift for description. Third, as a conversion narrative, the story makes a clear, inviting case for the need we all have for the intervention of grace in our lives. We learn that value and even salvation can come through raking as our weaknesses become strengths. In Charles's case, one of those weaknesses is his tendency to withdraw from, rather than draw closer to, others. His comparison of home teaching to raking, wherein we have an assigned friendship that forces us to interact with others and expand, rather than narrow, our associations and experiences, underscores the need for all of us to get outside our comfort zones and eschew the "impoverishment of experience" that is the end result of playing only to our strengths.

Like all stories of faith, this is a unique tale with echoes that will likely touch some aspect of our own lives. Charles, in taking the extremely courageous step to honestly open himself up to unknown readers from myriad places along the path, helps us all come to realize that we are not alone in the world. This narrative shows us that the stories we have heard or read are but a small drop in the wide ocean of spiritual experience that is part of the human legacy.

J. Scott Miller

CHAPTER 1

An Early Prayer

WAR COMES. MY FATHER'S FAMILY IN CALIFORNIA AND MY mother's family in Washington are sent to the same camp in Heart Mountain, Wyoming. There my parents meet and marry. When the fighting is over, they are free to live elsewhere.

They settle on a farm three miles west of Sigurd, Utah. The wind blows dust into our valley from the nuclear testing grounds in Nevada to the west. My sister Charlotte comes home from school one afternoon with bruises on her legs. Within months, she is dead. Blood cancer.

Age six.

I am born a year later. June 11, 1954.

My parents name me Charles, after my father. But as I learn more about Charlotte's death, I begin to wonder. Was I named after *her?*

Warren, friend Ishida Masami, Dillon, Dwight, Grandpa, Charles, and Annie on the Sigurd farm, ca. 1955.

I am falling. My father is driving a Farmall H tractor. My brother Warren and I are riding on the back. We hit a bump. I lose my grip. I land head first on the hay mower behind us. The steel crossbar splits my scalp open, but I survive.

I writhe on the operating table. "You're trying to hurt me!"

I turn my face away from the ether mask and from the men who are trying to hold me down.

My forehead is gashed at the hairline, my skull indented. For years afterward, my mother covers the scar with mascara.

We travel to California. I am four, far smaller than the tortoises at the San Diego Zoo. We stay at my Aunt Ruth's home in Chula Vista. One night, I dream that a building-sized monster is chasing me. It tries to crush me underfoot as I leap from mushroom to mushroom. I awake and go to where my father and mother are sleeping.

"A nightmare," my mother explains. "It will go away if you pray."

She sends me back to my bed. I fall on my knees and plead with my Heavenly Father to forgive me for the bad things I did that day. "Please take this nightmare from me."

I naturally believe that my nightmares are a result of my bad behavior and that God will make them go away if I ask for forgiveness.

I rest soundly until morning.

My mother, Bessie Shizuko Murakami, and my father, Charles Ichirō Inouye, have come to Utah in order to be far from the people who betrayed them. Most of the others trickle back to the West Coast after being released from internment. But not my family.

Living in an isolated desert valley, red mountains to the west, blue mountains to the east, my parents grow carrots and cabbage. Water for their fields comes from melted snow, brought down from the mountains by a system of rivers, reservoirs, and canals.

One summer, a pounding thunderstorm comes. A flash flood rushes down from the red cliffs of Cedar Ridge. The blood-red water overflows the canal and covers the earth near our house.

The next morning, I find huge, glistening fish stranded by the receding water.

> after the flood—
> three golden carp swimming on
> a gravel road

By noon, the water has seeped into the thirsty ground. The fish gasp for breath and die. The next day, their stench fills the air.

Our neighbors are Latter-day Saints. Like my parents, they, too, were driven from their homes by people who despised them. We came from west to east. They came from east to west, from New

York, Ohio, Missouri, and Illinois. A common fate brings us to the parched sage and cedar valleys of the Great Basin.

When Charlotte passes away, our Latter-day Saint neighbors offer the use of their small chapel for her funeral. During the service, my mother feels the Spirit. A seed of faith is planted in her heart. But out of respect for my grandparents, she postpones her embrace of this new god.

For generations, my ancestors have been Pure Land Buddhists (*Jōdo shinshū*). My grandfather Inouye Sashichi is a believer, but my father is not. He studied Marxism and social science in college and considers himself a "free thinker," "a peasant intellectual." He is bitter about the Relocation that robbed him of his home and business. He tells us, "What the War taught me is that you can't trust people. You can only trust ideas."

I find this odd. Aren't ideas what make people dangerous? Decades later, I write *Archipelago—Figurality and the Development of Modern Consciousness* in order to address the questions planted in my mind by my father's idealism. What is the phenomenon that we call "modernity"? And how did it come to control us with its tremendous, terrible concepts?

> hear the robins sing!
> making worlds of my own
> in a sandbox

CHAPTER 2

The Sigurd Ward, Sugar Cookies, Zen

THERE ARE NO OTHER JAPANESE FAMILIES FOR MILES AROUND. And the nearest Buddhist temple is in Salt Lake City, over two hours north by car. My parents want us to have some kind of spiritual training, but there are few possibilities in south-central Utah. Faced with this limitation, they dress us up every Sunday and take us into Sigurd. They drop us off in front of the Latter-day Saint chapel and come back two hours later to pick us up.

Occasionally my mother visits our classes. I'm not sure why. To give us support? To monitor what is being taught?

Whatever her motivations, her visits fill me with pride and comfort. I love to see her quietly sitting on a folding chair in the corner—shiny black hair, red lipstick, a form-fitting skirt.

*

Our Sigurd neighbors are from northern Europe. They have come to Utah from Denmark, Sweden, and England. The Dastrups, Jensens, Warnocks, Snedegars, and Jorgensons are friendly and welcoming. Perhaps my American experience is unique. Even in this land of genocide and slavery, I feel no prejudice from these people. I am blessed in this way.

*

These Latter-day Saints are good people. But I *am* afraid of Sister Miriam Dastrup, who leads a no-nonsense Junior Sunday School. She is the matriarch of the huge Dastrup clan. Tall and gray-haired, firm yet caring, she stands in front of a room of children and demands respect. She wants us to be faithful and obedient.

I don't pay much attention to what she's saying. My left shoulder is pressed against the plastered wall of the small room where we meet to sing and hear two-and-a-half-minute talks. I reach up and out. I touch the cool, uneven surface with my right hand.

"Charles, stop writing on the wall!" Sister Dastrup reprimands me.

"I'm not writing. I don't have a pencil," I defend myself.

"You're writing with your finger," she responds.

I wonder, "Is that possible?" But I don't argue with her. Already, I'm learning how to have questions that I keep to myself.

> Homo erectus—
> Adam and God touch fingers
> somewhere in Italy

*

The cottonwood trees outside the church are broad and tall. Planted by the pioneers, they drop a two-foot blanket of leaves in the fall. While waiting for the school bus, my sister Annie and I gather the musty leaves into huge mounds and dive into them.

One November day, after the leaves have been raked and taken away, I climb one of the trees next to the church. Chilled and stripped by the wind, the branch on which I sit provides a new—dare I say, modern?—perspective on the world.

> a cold October—
> a hen pheasant hides herself
> in a weed-choked ditch

6

Latter-day Saints are not Protestants, yet the church where we worship is simple in line. In 1820, when Joseph Smith went into the Sacred Grove to pray, he asked a modern question: Which of the many churches vying for his attention was true? The answer he received, though, was not modern at all. He was visited by two gods who had bodies, spoke to him directly, and knew him by name.

Given the physical glory of this first vision, one would expect to see more visual elaboration in Latter-day Saint buildings. But the church building in Sigurd is as plain as a pancake. No candles. No incense. No tales in colored glass. No carvings. No statues. There is only one painting—of Jesus in the Garden of Gethsemane. His clasped hands rest on top of a boulder. His eyes look upward in prayer.

The only other image in the building is a purple banner on which are written two words in gold letters: "BE REVERENT."

> through the desert air
> comes singing from the chapel—
> knapweed and the moon

I am alone much of the time, often lost in thought. The isolation of the farm reinforces both my imagination and my shyness. Until I go off to school, I have no one to play with other than my siblings. Even the well-spaced, fine-rooted *Juniperus utahensis* that grow in the shale-mounded foothills enjoy more companionship than I do.

I'm starved for friends. Fortunately, because my grandfather Inouye lives with us, my aunts, uncles, and cousins come to visit. I can count on seeing everyone a few days a year: Memorial Day, the opening day of trout season, Thanksgiving, Christmas, New Year's, and my grandfather's birthday in February. What joy I feel when my cousins arrive! We play until exhausted. This closeness to cousins lasts an entire lifetime and will get passed on to the next generation.

Every May, we take flowers to Charlotte's grave. We grieve together beneath the dry blue sky. Members of the National Guard fire their rifles into the air. From them, I learn the sound of shooting and the smell of gun powder.

> roses for Charlotte—
> scrambling for spent rifle shells
> among the graves

*

In June my father puts us in sleeping bags in the back of his pickup truck. We leave for the mountains in the middle of the night and arrive at Fish Lake at first light.

> the thick aspen groves
> hide the water from our view—
> a clear cold morning

*

Sometimes for Christmas we drive north to Salt Lake City. So many streets and houses. We sleep on the floor together, cousins.

> *otoshidama*—
> Uncle Mike gives us each a
> twenty-dollar bill

I have three brothers and two sisters. We span ten years from oldest to youngest.

1. Dillon Kazuyuki (the charismatic one)
2. [Charlotte Sachiko] (the angelic one)
3. Dwight Hideo (the quiet one)
4. Warren Sanji (the restless one)
5. Elizabeth Ann (my beloved Annie)
6. Charles Shirō (the fourth son, 四郎)

*

I have an easy smile. I laugh a lot and cry a lot. Being the youngest of six, I am sometimes favored, more often ignored.

We Inouye children grow up in two very different worlds. While at church and at school, we live like our *hakujin* neighbors. Like them, we speak English. We eat school lunch, even the very foreign rice pudding and creamed spinach. At home, Kikkōman soy sauce and the twanging shamisen of my grandfather's vinyl records rule.

My ancestors are from Kyushu, Japan's southern island. My father's father and my mother's mother are still alive. They live with us—my grandfather all the time, and my grandmother about six months a year. They are Issei. They speak only Japanese. My Nisei parents talk to them in Japanese and to us in English. We Sansei children speak only English.

Me, kuchi, hana (eyes, mouth, nose). Grandfather teaches us a few words of Japanese whenever we sleep together. But other than that, there is little foreign language learning in our home. My parents don't encourage it. They want us to be American.

*

My mother cooks many different kinds of food. Teriyaki chicken, beef curry, chow mein, stuffed peppers, tuna noodle casserole, pancakes with beaten egg whites folded into the batter.

From my grandmother Kume's garden come cantaloupes, watermelons, lettuce, zucchini, tomatoes, corn, *nappa, daikon*, string beans, beets.

"Horse manure is the best fertilizer," she tells us.

The one thing my mother doesn't do is bake. Baking is what Latter-day Saint women do. We eat no bread from mother's oven until many years later, when Sister Nedra Stewart invites my mother to her home and teaches her the secrets of bread making.

9

To be a true Latter-day Saint, you have to bake. Gifts from the family oven—loaves of bread and plates of cookies—are common expressions of love.

Christmas is days away. The Sigurd Ward is having its annual party. The folding chairs are stacked along the walls. Everyone mingles and dances.

I am a sheep in the nativity program.

Toward the end of the evening, everyone is given a sugar cookie.

I can't believe my good fortune. I get one, just like everyone else. My cookie is huge and covered with pink frosting. I bite into it. How rich and sweet! Its generous taste confirms to me, as the Primary song goes, that "I am a child of God." Even members of my family, even me. What joy to know that the people of Sigurd are my brothers and sisters!

Even now I remember the taste of that cookie.

In the Book of Mormon, Lehi sees the tree of life. Its fruit is "sweet, above all that [he] ever before tasted." It fills his soul "with exceedingly great joy" and is "desirable above all" (1 Nephi 8:11–12).

Later, his son Nephi asks to see the same dream and to be taught its meaning. He is told by angels that the tree and its fruit are the love of God.

In their great poverty, the women of Sigurd, Utah, teach me this same vision. They introduce me to this same sweetness. They are my angels. They are the many heads and hands of Kannon the Compassionate. When Kannon contemplated the misery of this world, her head exploded. But then it grew back, and she had eleven heads with twenty-two eyes to see even more misery. In response, Amida gave her extra arms with extra hands, to reach out and help those in need. With their work-thickened palms, the sisters of Sigurd shaped the cookies that filled my soul with a sweetness that lingers to this day. How could I ever forget their kindness?

> sisters of Sigurd—
> the gift of sugar cookies
> lard, flour, sugar, and salt

The smell of Mormonism is the aroma of baked goods. The smell of Buddhism is the scent of smoldering sandalwood. For better or worse, both scents shape my understanding of the world. Zion Earth Zen Sky. I walk the horizon where they meet, not knowing which is up and which is down.

As a child, I am afraid of many things. I am especially haunted by the moaning wind. It brought the poison dust that killed my sister. It tells me that I am alone. One stormy afternoon, the gusts tug at the screen door. I go to my grandfather and cling to his pant leg.

He leads me into his bedroom. He pulls a chair up to his dresser. He stands me on it, facing the Buddhist altar. He puts an agate-beaded rosary in my hands. He lights two sticks of incense and rings a tarnished brass bell.

"*Namu Amida Butsu*" (Praise to Amida).

"*Namu Amida Butsu*," I repeat the words.

In the back of the altar is a small black-and-white photo. It stands next to the image of Amida. Years later, I learn that the woman in the picture is my grandmother. Inouye Mikano, a woman I never met, whispers to me. "Don't let me be forgotten."

Her only son was my father, whom she loved dearly. I later learn that it was she, not my grandfather, who gave Charles Ichirō Inouye his coat of many colors. With her devotion and with her great hopes for his success, she planted a seed of greatness in his heart, along with a seed of anguish.

> two sticks of incense—
> tendrils of scented smoke rise
> to the dark ceiling

Along with Pure Land Buddhism, Zen is the other Mahayana sect that flourished most notably in Japan. For hundreds of years, my Kyushu ancestors have been affiliated with the Honshōji, a temple near the Chikugo River in Amagi. Being samurai, my ancestors would have also been familiar with Zen teachings and practices.

Both Jōdo and Zen gave life and mystery to the Noh theater, an art form patronized by the warrior class. In these stately plays, death becomes life, and the trauma of murder is healed by the turning wheel, the law, the dharma.

> young Atsumori,
> "I am not your enemy"—
> Amida's kind grace

Residing at a level still deeper than Buddhism is the native Japanese belief that all things have a spirit. As I will write in *Evanescence and Form*, animism is the ancient (and still continuing) foundation of Japanese culture. As a mixture of both animism and Buddhism, Zen is perhaps the most Japanese of all Mahayana sects because it allows itself to be deeply influenced by the power of things.

Mono—もの, 物, 者, モノ. Japanese things are both inanimate and animate, singular and plural, intangible and material. *Kimono*— a thing to wear. *Tabemono*—a thing to eat. *Warumono*—a bad person.

The genius of Zen is the genius of restored Christianity. Both bring the abstract concepts of heaven down to earth. Both make the ordinary things of this world the way (道) to salvation.

sadō (the way of tea) 茶道
kohdō (the way of incense) 香道
kendō (the way of the sword) 剣道
kadō (the way of flower arrangement) 花道
jūdō (the pliant way of defensive fighting) 柔道

These *dō* (道) are Zen paths. Each one yields spiritual knowledge by way of physical practice—arranging flowers, serving tea, and so on. The forms (*kata*) that give them order are repeated until they become second nature, until rocks become water, and people become one with the gods.

For Latter-day Saints, it is much the same. Our training is short on theology and long on practice. Our philosophical accomplishments are few, and our practical victories many. During my lifetime, the lyrics of "I Am a Child of God" are changed from "teach me all that I must know" to "teach me all that I must do."

From an early age, we are taught to be rakers, to be constantly practicing our values. The ten gardens of Latter-day Saint life are these.

tithing
service to others
daily exercise and rest
the sacrament on Sunday
daily study and meditation
family home evening each week
temple attendance when possible
wholesome recreation
constant prayer
proper diet

As with Zen, understanding comes to Latter-day Saints by doing the same things over and over and over. Yes, the pilgrim's progress is modest. But, as Confucius says, "Is it not joy when an old friend comes from afar?" We perceive the subtle changes that

13

happen in our hearts—here a little, there a little—only because the lessons we learn in our youth, our old friends, are unchanging. They visit from time to time and show us how much we have progressed.

God's commandments are the *kata* of life. By obedience to them, we become aware of the truth of evanescence and of the life-giving miracle of the Atonement.

Some Zen practitioners believe in quick enlightenment. Others think understanding comes slowly. In either case, the focus is on overcoming the self by way of constant practice.

> Christian Zen—
> the Forest of Keta (気多) has
> never seen an ax

At the Kennin Temple in Kyoto, there is an ancient Zen rock garden. Here gravel is carefully raked into geometric patterns and punctuated with rocks and moss. Trees grow around the edges. The sight of it makes you ask the same question that comes to mind when viewing the sprawling gardens at Versailles.

"How is such a thing possible?"

It is the same query in either place. But the answers—one modern and one not—are never more different than when asked in these two locations. The beauty of Versailles is vast and grand, the magnificence of perspective, of the "big picture." In comparison, the beauty of the Kenninji is small and contained. The concrete splendor of the rock garden is the "small picture."

I show both—big and small gardens—to my students. I pose a question. What is the difference between the beauty of one god (and one kingdom) and of many gods (and many kingdoms)? Although often misunderstood, the Latter-day truths of Zion are

14

more like the small truths of Zen than like the big truths of traditional Christianity.

> in the desert—
> the rocks are warm with rain
> and the sky is blue

The carefully raked gravel of Kenninji requires involvement and constant attention. Whenever a maple leaf or a pine needle falls onto the sand, the garden needs to be raked again. Day after day. Week after week. Year after year. Care must be given because perfection never lasts.

Gardens like this are high maintenance. While their upkeep might seem like a waste of time and effort, this requirement to "waste time" is precisely their usefulness to us. The garden reminds us that our lives, too, are high maintenance. We have no choice but to rake and rake. Every day, without ceasing.

If we are to be whole, if we are to maintain our sanity, if we are to be compassionate, we have to constantly practice our ideals.

The Zen garden at the Kenninji, in Kyoto, Japan.

Without doing so, all would soon be lost, and the purpose of our lives forgotten.

Another way to say this is that we can never be fixed, once and for all. In our victories, the seeds of decay are planted. Rocks become soil. Kindness becomes pride and neglect. But the presence of anything ordered and complex means that interventions of design and intelligence are being made just as continually as decay. The influence of a loving Creator is so obvious that we are blind to it. Does a bird think of air? A fish think of water?

Without trials, we would have no awareness of anything valuable. In this world, we live "by the sweat of our brow." Against the steady pull of decline and chaos, we rake. At first, our lines are irregular and imperfect. But with practice, the patterns of our divinity emerge with a simple beauty.

Without this constant effort, we would give in to lust, ambition, and pride. No one is beyond the need to rake. Even someone so gifted as J. Robert Oppenheimer cried, driveled, spat, and sweated his way through life. What did his brilliance find? A fine hat? A way to kill thousands of people at a time?

> Hiroshima—
> our precise world is made of
> imprecise sand

Sooner or later, we learn. Our days are full of sorrow. They pass quickly. There is no time to waste.

Yesterday's beauty is gone today. Something always happens to mar perfection. Something always destroys our happiness. How sobering it is to say, "We were happy." We hide in our secrets. Lovers fight and separate. How terrible! The constant breakdown of things from complex to simple is trying.

But if raking teaches us about decline, it also awakens us to growth. In this world of chaos, trees grow. Children mature. Our world has the potential to flourish. What lasts is not Babel or the grandeur of Versailles. It is God's love. Thankfully, the smallness of the Zen garden saves us. It invites us to participate, not to stand back and look. The smallest acts of kindness release the immense power of the universe.

The Buddhists call this state of compassion nothingness. Unlike Oppenheimer, Nagarjuna used his intelligence to help us understand the limits of brilliance. His logic proved that we cannot conceive of the self without a conception of no-self. If self depends on no-self, we can't say it exists on its own. It is contingent, as is everything else. Nothing exists on its own. Everything is connected.

From the *Heart Sutra*, we read, "Form is no different from emptiness. Emptiness is no different from form." 色不異空、空不異色.

> springtime nothingness—
> picking grass and plantains from
> the slowly growing moss

We are constantly fixing, mending, and patching. Our homes are Zen gardens that require endless cleaning. Righteous men need admirers. Virtuous women demand diamonds and pearls. But in Zion earth and Zen sky, we work hard to get nowhere. There is no accomplishment, no acclaim, no fame, no fortune.

Climbing to +1 would result in a fall to -1. Only at 0 is there equilibrium and harmony. Zion is zero. Where our hearts are one, where there are no poor. East of Eden, there is nowhere to go except where we are. There is no one to be but who we are.

And who are we if not outcasts from paradise?

We wander. We stumble upon the truth. T. S. Elliot understood the journey, and the emptiness of it all. "We shall not cease from exploration, and the end of all our exploring will be to arrive where we started and know the place for the first time." Our journey takes us back to where we began, back to where we started to happen.

Jesus called it a "child's mind." The Buddhists call it "no-mind."

*

We start in "the burning house." Being a part of the world, it, too, is a site of constant change, *samsara*. Why, then, is it a place most of us would not want to do without? Home is our treasure, our place of safety. Yet it is of all places the most dangerous and limiting.

Someone invites us to a party next door. We step out into the street. Only then do we see smoke and flames showing at the second-floor window. Only then do we realize that "yes, my house is on fire."

Leaving home, we begin our search for the truth. We look for a new source of comfort. We learn the difference between right and wrong. We choose the right. We climb toward god, toward truth, toward reality. Our progress is exhilarating. We are learning cause and effect. We see how good brings about good and how bad brings about bad.

But then, just as we are about to enjoy our hard-earned happiness, we begin to understand the limitations of justice. To our great surprise, we learn that justice leads us to sorrow instead of to happiness. We come to understand that all people are fallible, and that the last thing we really want is for everyone to get what they deserve. We begin to feel the sadness of all things—*mono no aware*, as Motoori Norinaga put it—a deep sorrow that justice cannot cure.

This is when a second turning, a second conversion, must happen. Surprised by the world's sorrow, most of us give up and resign ourselves to live in a state of justice. But some follow their heart. They move ahead, deeper into sorrow, on to compassion. Like Abraham and Noah and Moses, they bargain with God and turn away from their idols of Truth—not to ignore him, but to become like him, faced *toward* suffering, not *away* from the burning house.

Without this second conversion, the world would slip away. With this second turn, we begin our descent, our condescension.

Like Jesus, like Amida, like Kannon, we choose to remain in a world filled with suffering. We go back to the burning house to save those who are still there.

After all, what good is my salvation if Uncle Bob is still on the couch, watching television and eating chips? For him, we throw a party—like the one that was thrown for us. For him, we mediate, we intercede, we invite him to begin the journey that ultimately leads beyond justice to compassion.

Why is justice not enough? Can we do without justice?

No. But justice is like food. We can't live without it. But too much kills us.

One afternoon, we gather together on the hardwood stage in the Sigurd chapel. The teachers tug at the heavy black curtains, pulling this way and that. They create a pocket of space just big enough for a teacher and three children.

For some reason, I pay attention to the lesson that day.

When our teacher asks questions about what she's taught, I can answer them all. I raise my hand, and she calls on me. Once, twice, three times.

I say this not to brag, but to make a point. When we want to learn, we can, and do. The Spirit comes pouring in.

CHAPTER 3

First Corruptions, School, Rescue

It is early spring. The air is chilly. Snowstorms move through the valley.

My parents plant cabbage seeds in hotbeds made of pine. On cold nights, they cover the long rectangular boxes with lengths of white cotton cloth to make a womb. My grandfather waters the sprouting plants every morning with a hose and a spray nozzle. When the seedlings are two inches tall, they are taken to the fields and transplanted.

In late summer, with the first cool air, the hard heads of cabbage are cut and placed into rows. We load them onto wagons and store them in a large underground cellar. They are later bagged and taken to market in huge eighteen-wheeled semitrucks.

*

Standing near the entrance to the cabbage cellar, I watch one of the eighteen-wheelers slowly back into the earth. The giant snake enters the hole, tail first. The tires turn slowly backwards. The brakes hiss, and the behemoth comes to a stop. The tractor is still out in the bright sunlight, but the long aluminum trailer has entered the darkness of the pit.

While my father and his crew load squeaky fifty-pound sacks of cabbage into the rear of the trailer, I am free to roam.

I walk into the sunlight, up to the front of the truck. The chrome lug nuts gleam, as do the headlights and mirrors. Even the windows sparkle in the morning light. The powerful diesel engine idles calmly, patiently. It waits for the driver to return.

I come around to the door. It's slightly open.

Since the driver is helping with the loading, I decide to scale the steps and crawl into the cab.

Suddenly, I'm in a space capsule, about to blast off to the moon! The gauges on the dashboard, the smoothness of the steering wheel, the hardness of the gearshift knobs, the stale smell of cigarette smoke—everything is new and exciting.

Sitting in the driver's seat, I am too small to reach the pedals with my feet or to see over the steering wheel.

But I can stare at the dangling keys and listen to the idling engine. Minutes pass as the loading of the trailer continues behind me.

My mind is racing. I get to my knees and look out the windows. In the rearview mirror, the trailer seems to have been swallowed by the earth. Occasionally, I feel a quiver, as the men continue loading the trailer with cabbage.

I hear a voice of warning. "Leave! Now!"

But the curtain that hangs between the two seats encourages me to explore.

I discover a small sleeping area for the driver back there.

I enter.

In the sudden darkness, I see a mattress, a blanket, a pillow. Sunlight leaks through the small round portholes at the head and foot of the bed. In the dim light, I notice that the walls and ceiling are covered with photographs of naked women.

They are everywhere.

My heart starts pounding. My face grows hot.

Minutes later, I make my way out to the driver's seat. I slide down the steps to the ground. I run from the truck, the images burned into my mind.

Too embarrassed to tell anyone about what has happened, I let secrecy begin to drive me deeper into the prison of my slowly forming self.

> reverently now
> I close my eyes in prayer—
> smooth skin shiny hair

In the silence of the Utah countryside, I fill the quiet hours alone, wandering outdoors. I find heavy metal objects and try to pick them up. I want to be strong. Someday I will be able to pick up anything. I tell myself, "Someday, I will be strong."

I climb trees. I play dolls with my sister, Annie.

> beyond the wooden fence—
> abandoned trucks, tumbleweeds,
> weathered deer antlers

> thick green willows—
> a meadowlark sings by an
> irrigation ditch

In my mind I'm often a warrior, wielding a sword or braving a winter storm. Just as often, I imagine I'm in love. When that happens, I'm a girl.

I'm not sure why. But yin is more romantic than yang.

*

I flatten myself beneath the cool sheets of my bed. It would be wonderful to be Nancy Dastrup—to have her long wavy brown hair, her brilliant smile. She is one of the young women of the Sigurd Ward. I'm convinced that everyone would love me if I were her. Annie and I spend many hours playing Nancy.

Does the love of God require anything harder than this—for boys to imagine the heart of girls and for girls to know the heart of boys?

> of sticks and stones—
> raindrops roll off the dry ground
> into the small stream

Inouye Taniyuki, my cousin from Japan, comes to America to work on the farm.

His first lesson is to learn how to drive.

With Taniyuki at the wheel, everyone is standing around the 1952 GMC pickup—my father and mother, my brothers and sister. I find a place directly behind the truck. Wondering what it looks like underneath, I get down on my knees to take a look.

Next thing I know, I'm back at the hospital in Richfield. Except for a few pieces of gravel embedded in my back, there is no evidence of being run over by the truck. For a second time, my life is spared.

Every year, a few Navajo families come north from the reservation in Arizona. The Johns, the Begays, the Manygoats. They thin sugar beets in the spring and pick potatoes in the fall. One year, upon their return to Arizona, Alice John takes the foot-powered Singer sewing machine that she has borrowed from my mother. When asked about it, Alice agrees to make my mother a rug in order to pay her back.

Over the next few weeks, I watch the entire process of Alice's repentance. She sets up a log frame. She cards and dyes wool sheared from the skins of the sheep her family have killed and eaten. She spins the yarn and begins weaving a rug. Before my eyes, a web of black, brown, and white wool becomes a universe of sacred mountains and endless deserts.

Sisnaajina—
strands of wool turn into
sacred mountains

Annie is a year older than I am. When she starts going to school, my mother gives me the job of walking her to the bus stop. Every noon, we have chicken noodle soup and white bread with butter, then walk together past the haystack and out to the county road.

Annie's afraid of the haystack. "Robbers are waiting for us there," she says.

I am not bothered by many of the things that threaten her, and this qualifies me for my assignment: "Make sure Annie gets to the bus stop." I accept the mission. I want to be a hero. I want to help people.

One day, the bus is late.

Henry Timican, a Paiute man who works for my father, comes by on a tractor. I flag him down and ask for help. I leave Annie at the crossroads and catch a ride back to the house. Something's wrong. I have to tell my mother.

By the time we pull into the yard, the yellow bus is driving away in the distance, leaving behind a long trail of dust. Annie is safely on her way to school.

Mission accomplished.

dear sister Annie—
for you, my favorite sweater
is covered with grease

A year later, I'm riding that same bus. What joy! Now I will have people to play with. I'm self-conscious, though. My hands, elbows, and knees are black from constantly playing in the dirt. No matter how hard I wash, the darkness of my skin remains.

My kindergarten class at Ashman Elementary in Richfield, Utah.

By October, my heart is pounding. I've just fallen in love with a girl named Sally McBride. She has shiny brown hair and a bright, gap-toothed smile. I invite her to be my partner in the upcoming Halloween parade, and she accepts.

*

The thought of walking with her, hand in hand, thrills me! But what will I be for Halloween? I spot a devil costume in the window of the variety store in Richfield. I need it. Sally will love me if I'm the devil.

But my mother has another idea. "We'll make you something."

*

Each morning at school, Sally reports. It's always something new—a diadem, a tutu, pink shoes stitched with purple sequins. She's going to be a ballerina.

"And what are *you* going to be?"

Each time, the question fills me with agony. When I return home, I ask my mother Sally's question. And each time there is no answer. It's harvest season, and everyone is busy. As the Japanese idiom goes, my parents would hire a cat if one came along.

Every day at school, Sally keeps asking, "What are you going to be?"

And each time I tell her, "It's a surprise."

This deception seems to make her more interested in me. But it only makes me more miserable.

I don't know who I'm going to be.

On the day before the parade, I am so discouraged that I don't bother to pester my mother anymore. I am without hope. I am a dog without paws.

*

Dinner is over. My mother turns to me. "Well, aren't you going to ask us something?"

I shake my head. I feel empty inside.

"No questions?"

"No. I don't care."

I stare at the tabletop. There's a discolored, chipped part of the Formica, where someone put a hot kettle down on it.

"You don't care?"

"No."

"Well, come and see."

*

My mother leads me into the next room. She produces a set of thermal underwear, a cotton hood, some socks, a pair of short pants. Everything is colored with the same green Rit dye.

"Put these on."

"What is it?"

"Go ahead. Try them on."

"What is it?"

"See if you can guess."

I do as I'm told. Now I'm green, from head to toe. But I still don't have a clue about what I'm supposed to be.

27

"Well. What do you think?"

I shrug my shoulders.

My father goes to the closet. He brings out a disc-shaped object. It's made from a metal loop with chicken wire and canvas stretched over the whole thing, like a giant contact lens dyed green.

I notice two straps. One for each shoulder? "Oh, no." I think to myself. "I'm a turtle."

*

The next day, I board the bus. My head sags. I'm embarrassed. At school, I stuff my turtle costume in the corner of the classroom. When it's time to get ready for the parade, I face the wall, away from everybody.

I put on my green underwear. When I finally turn around, she's there. Sally's walking my way!

She's beaming with happiness. Dressed in her new ballerina costume, she is lovely beyond description. How can anyone be so pretty? The tutu, the diadem, the dancing shoes sparkling with sequins—everything is perfect. Her walnut-colored hair swirls around her face. She smiles.

Facing her, I wish I could turn into air and blow out the window. Why am I not a devil—store-bought, shiny red, with a mask and triton?

"What are you?"

She asks the question.

I'm too ashamed to answer. Words are a clump of rice stuck in my throat.

"You're . . ."

I look down at the floor.

"A turtle, right?"

I don't say anything. My embarrassment is total.

"How cute!"

I look up. I'm confused.

"You're *so* cute!" she says.

Have I misheard her? "You mean you like my costume?"

"I do," she says. "It's darling."

Turns out, Sally loves my turtle outfit, as do all the people of Richfield, Utah. As we parade down the street—princess and turtle—they point and smile. "Oh, look at that. How cute."

I spot my mother standing in the crowd. She looks worried. But when she sees me smiling, her expression changes.

I wave. "Hi, mom!"

She waves back and smiles.

How fortunate I am to have a caring mother.

Both life's sorrow and beauty manifest themselves in the difference between the Japanese verb *aru*, "to be, to have, there is," and its *-gatai* conjugation, as in *arigatai*, "difficult to be, hard to have, rare." I give thanks for what makes life possible even as the indebtedness I feel toward others becomes heavy and hard to bear. *Arigatai n' desu.*

Jesus died so we can live. How can I ever repay him for the feelings of forgiveness that I enjoy? Amida, too, is always there for me and my family, with his warm, bright rays of mercy extending in every direction.

Arigatō gozaimasu. I thank the gods for making my life possible, including the gods of earth and sky, of trees and rocks. All things are animated with God's power. To everything in this world, he gives design and intelligence. With his rake, the world was created. With ours, it is maintained.

As I grow older, I start to spend more time with my father. Despite the dangers of farming, he likes to take me along.

And I like to go with him because I admire his active life. He is a manly man, a Kyushu man. He skillfully operates in the world of things—cedar posts, shovelfuls of mud, grease guns, nuts and bolts. By his example, he teaches me that there is *always* a way to accomplish whatever we set out to do.

One morning, we are cleaning an irrigation ditch full of weeds and silt. I am sitting on the MD tractor, where I've been ordered to "stay put." Farming can be dangerous, as I already know. If I fall from that tractor, it's a long way to the ground.

My father is standing on the ditcher that the tractor is pulling, trying to adjust the angle at which its large iron V bites into the earth. I hear a sound and see a movement. My dad suddenly screams out. His foot is trapped between two crossbars of steel. He struggles to free himself. But he's trapped.

He calls to me. His voice is filled with pain, but he struggles to stay calm. "Charlie, I need some help."

"Okay."

"There in front of you. Two levers. See them?"

"Right here?" I point.

He nods. "Listen. My foot is trapped, and I need you to get me out. Can you do it?"

"I'll try."

"I want you to push the top lever in and pull the bottom one out. But you have to do both at the same time. Push the top, pull the bottom. At exactly at the same time. Understand?"

I'm afraid, but I need to be brave.

"I'm going to count to three. When I say "three," push the top one in and pull the bottom one out. Got it?"

"I think so."

"You're going to have to do it as hard as you can."

"Okay."

"One. Two. Three!"

I give it all I have. I push the top lever and pull the bottom one. The idling tractor shudders and the hydraulic cylinder on the ditcher expands, releasing pressure on my father's foot. Freed from the trap, he falls to the ground.

Thirty seconds later, he stands up in the weeds. He limps over to where I am still sitting on the tractor seat.

"Good boy."

He climbs up, and we immediately head for home.

My mother soaks my father's crushed foot in a bucket of warm water and Epsom salts. It's bruised and purple, but Mom says he's going to be all right.

Sitting there, facing her in the middle of the kitchen, my father tells the story of how I worked the levers. "I wouldn't have made it home without Charlie."

I'm a hero.

From this point forward, I am fiercely loyal to my father.

Only many years later do I realize that had the hydraulic cylinder retracted rather than expanded, the ditcher's steel crossbars would have crushed my father's foot off.

CHAPTER 4

Gunnison, My Road to Damascus, A Tragic Weakness

I AM BAPTIZED. AGE EIGHT.

Dillon, who is old enough to perform the ordinance, forgets to say "Amen" after the prayer.

We do it over again.

> Ana baptism—
> I die more than once to
> live with God again

One morning, my father drives into Richfield to get some parts at the NAPA Auto Parts store.

By the time he's done talking with the men at the counter, I'm already late for school.

We pull up in front of Ashman Elementary. I pop open the door and start running across the lawn toward the schoolhouse. I get about fifty yards when I hear my father calling.

"Charlie!"

I stop. I turn around and run back to the car.

I stick my head in the opened window. "What?"

"Don't be afraid to be different," he says.

"Okay." I nod, turn around, and start running across the lawn again.

I have no idea what my father is trying to tell me. Only when I am much older do I learn the importance of this moment. I am different. My father wants to prepare me for the challenges ahead.

In 1964 we move north thirty miles to a town called Gunnison. We start buying land to the west of town, where a colony of Jewish settlers from Philadelphia once started a community on reclaimed ground just beneath the newly dug Paiute Canal. Apparently, none of them were farmers. They eventually failed and moved away. Others move in to give it a try.

We commute to the farm from a house in Gunnison, which is home to about two thousand people. There are no more than about twelve blocks in the entire town, but the roads connecting them are paved, and some have sidewalks. For the first time in my life, I ride my bike on something other than gravel.

> no greater joy—
> speeding down a smooth concrete
> sidewalk on my bike

My summers are spent weeding fields of sugar beets and potatoes. The sun beats down. The gnats and mosquitoes attack. As I walk up and down the fields, row after row, my mind seeks refuge from the tedium and discomfort.

Even though my body is enslaved to the task at hand, my imagination is free to roam. My thoughts take me to wherever they want to go.

I am now old enough to begin asking questions that I ponder for hours, even days at a time. Without knowing it, I'm training for the job I will eventually have as a professor—trying to solve impossibly difficult questions.

- If all the lost coins in the world were found, how many coins would there be?
- If you piled up the hair from all the haircuts that have ever been given, how big would that pile be?

As I grow older and approach puberty, my questions grow increasingly absurd.

- Is the sacrament a form of cannibalism?
- If people had three instead of two eyes, how different would the world be?

Without knowing it, my mind is inching toward the absurdity of the Zen *kōan*. These are difficult-to-answer questions designed to teach the limits of logic and reason. Their impossibility encourages us not to get lost in the world of ideas but to be present in this world of things.

- What is the sound of one hand clapping?
- Can a sharp sword cut itself?
- If a tree fell in the forest and no one was there to see it, could we say that a tree fell?

I later learn that there are set answers to these questions. To the question about one hand clapping, the answer is "one hand."

My intellectual development progresses at this beet-field pace. Maybe I would learn more quickly if I had more stimulation. To a certain point of view, the schools in rural Utah are not that rigorous. Gunnison Valley High School teaches home economics, wood shop, vocational agriculture, and seminary. But the only foreign language offered is English.

English is a foreign language to us because none of us speak or write it that well. All the sentences on the proficiency exams they make us take look pretty good to me.

Which is correct?

> a. Ten items or less.
> b. Ten items or fewer.
> c. Both a and b.
> d. Neither a nor b.

My father grew up in a shack that could be dismantled, transported, and put back up in a single day. Still, the public schools that California offered him were far better than the ones I'm attending in Utah. As a former valedictorian at Sequoia High School in Redwood City and as one of the first Japanese Americans to be admitted to Stanford University, my father is concerned enough about my future to give me some strong advice: "Charlie, people who don't read live one life. But people who read live many lives."

I must be hungry for many lives, because I start driving tractor by day and reading Dostoevsky by night. Little does my father know that by nudging me in the direction of literature, he's undoing his grand scheme to have me take over the farm someday.

I attend church on Sundays, but only when we're not working in the fields, which is not often. Some summers, I get as few as two or three days off.

I'm reading Dickens, Hesse, and Steinbeck. I'm beginning to feel life's competing agendas. I begin to see how consistency would require a narrowing of options. For instance, my Latter-day Saint teachers tell me that I should honor the Sabbath, attend church, and take the sacrament each week. But my father wants me to help him on the farm, even on Sundays. Which is it going to be? Work or worship? Obey my father on earth or be true to my Father in Heaven?

I arrange a meeting with Lamont Nielsen, first counselor to the bishop of the Gunnison First Ward. I explain my situation. "I want to attend church, but my father makes me work on Sundays. What should I do?"

Brother Nielsen, who is also a farmer, tilts his head to the side and takes his time coming to an answer. I hope he will say, "Honor the Sabbath, you fool." But he surprises me.

When he finally answers, he says in his always thoughtful, quiet voice, "Charles, I think you should do what your father asks you to do. Honor thy father and thy mother, that thy days may be long upon the land. Do this, and I promise you: things will work out someday."

Darn! I am disappointed. And not because my pious soul hungers and thirsts after righteousness. I just want a little break from farming once in a while. "Heavenly Father, is that too much to ask?"

One Sunday, I'm helping my father repair a ventilation unit in one of our potato pits. Potatoes are living things. Without enough oxygen, they will rot in storage.

We break for lunch. Typically, my mother puts two sandwiches, a bag of chips, and a pickle or piece of fruit in our lunch pails.

We are sitting in the pickup truck. It's a spring day—cold in the morning, warm in the afternoon. My father turns on the radio, which is always tuned to KSVC, the local station in Richfield. It's the only channel you can pick up clearly in my part of the world—that and KMTI in Manti. General conference is being broadcast from the Tabernacle in Salt Lake City. I'm thinking he'll turn the radio off. But no. Not only does he *not* turn it off, but he listens to the talks with great concentration.

Gunnison Valley, from the G hill looking south toward Salina.

"You mean, he's not hostile toward Christianity?" I think to myself.

It takes me a while to figure my father out. He's a complicated man.

> a father a son—
> searching the desert air for
> the one true station

I am growing up in the very heart of Mormondom. Most consider Salt Lake City the epicenter of The Church of Jesus Christ of Latter-day Saints. There the church has its tall office buildings, the Tabernacle, the temple. There the prophets live in houses with lawns, sprinklers, and rubber hoses. But the real ground zero of our faith is the Sevier River Valley to the south. Little has changed in the string of farm towns along the muddy river.

Brigham Young, the second prophet of the church, sent a number of families to settle this area. Here in the valleys of the mountains, the imaginative genius of Joseph Smith and the organizational brilliance of his successor are both still alive and in full tension with each other. Life is humble here and still as sweetly romantic as a loaf of bread with butter. To the north, the greener, richer part of the state has become more worldly and has lost this same simplicity.

*

German tourists visit southern Utah in rented campmobiles. They see our endless vistas and blue skies. They consider the weeds growing along the highway and exclaim, "*Wunderbar!*"

What they don't understand is that the beauty of our desert paradise is lethal.

Partly, it's because we country people live with so few distractions. No soundtrack plays in the background. There is little here to lure and distract us. There is only the quiet, dry air and the constant wind to deal with day after day.

Living in that silence, we either find god, develop an addiction, or kill ourselves. Just on my street alone, three people commit suicide.

I am a teenager. Many temptations come. Some of my schoolmates start drinking beer. I give it a try but never take to it. I feel no compulsion to break my promise not to drink.

My father has a stash of scotch under the sink. He tells me and my brothers, "You want to get drunk? Go ahead. I'll get whatever you want. Just don't go making a big show of it like your silly Mormon friends."

His open-mindedness pulls the plug on my instinct to rebel.

Slowly yet surely, I'm coming to understand who I am. By his example, my father is teaching me that one of the things I truly hate is hypocrisy.

I don't feel superior to my friends who party occasionally. People need a change of consciousness. It's just that I don't think I could get drunk on Saturday night and bless the sacrament on Sunday morning. No amount of soap and hot water could clean that grease from beneath my nails.

*

There's another way to put it: I'm becoming idealistic. It's the sixties, after all, and both idealism and decadence are twin ribbons dancing in the air. Often, they intertwine and tangle, like a string of beads around a silk scarf. I prefer the Beatles to the Rolling Stones, which means I am probably more Apollonian than Dionysian.

*

What I certainly am is stubborn. My father runs into my Scoutmaster at the post office. "You know, Mr. Inouye, your son Charles only has one merit badge to go to get his Eagle."

In response, my father, socialist at heart yet capitalist in practice, offers an incentive: "Charlie, I'll give you fifty dollars if you finish up."

I immediately stop going to Scouts. No one is going to bribe me. As I said, it's the sixties, and I'm learning how to fight "the system."

Many years later, I'm still proud of myself for holding to my standards as a teenager. But when I become a Scoutmaster and my son Leif earns his Eagle, I feel a tinge of regret for not being able to join him in the "Eagles' nest" at his court of honor.

> a world gone to hell—
> John Lennon gets murdered and
> Mick Jagger goes gray

Joseph Smith wrote that, as a young man "left to all kinds of temptations; and, mingling with all kinds of society, [he] frequently fell into many foolish errors . . . offensive in the sight of God" (Joseph Smith History—1:28).

I, too, begin to "mingle with all kinds of society." I, too, commit "many foolish errors . . . offensive in the sight of God." My weaknesses are legion. But of all my faults, there is one that is particularly troubling.

My brother Dwight points it out to me. "You avoid things. You stay away from people you don't like."

He's right. That's exactly it. Dwight sees me correctly and pointedly, in the way that only an older brother can see a younger brother.

My greatest single weakness is that I steer clear of people and situations that challenge me.

Maybe "shy" doesn't quite capture it. I'm not just shy. My problem is something deeper and more serious. I keep my distance from things that make me feel uncomfortable. I avoid people and situations that force me to adjust my values. I am easily hurt by criticism. I judge others.

I don't know exactly why I'm like this. Maybe it's for the same reasons that I laugh and cry so easily. I have a sensitive heart. Maybe I'm trying to protect myself by keeping a distance from those who are different from me, even as I hunger for companionship and friendship, even as I am driven by my hero complex to reach out to others, even as I want to love everyone.

The problem with my propensity to withdraw is that it gets in the way of empathy and understanding. I might have a tender heart and an easy smile. But tenderness without connection is like a swimmer without water. Until I learn to overcome this weakness, my soft heart is of little use to me or to anyone else. It is, in fact, crippling.

A Buddhist would say that my problem is that I don't understand *anatman*—the truth of no self. There is no such thing as the "I" that I worry about so much. In truth, there really is no soul to protect, nowhere to run to, no person to be. It will take me a long time to understand the nothingness of all things. It will take me many cycles of sin and repentance to understand that the world is filled with God's love, even to the point that I do not exist except as a manifestation of that love.

As a result of my personal weakness, terrible things happen. For example, had it not been for my delusional sense of self, a Navajo man might not have died.

It happened this way.

One day in June, he comes to the farm, driving a Chevy pickup. He's broke. He needs work.

My father has him haul hay with me.

I drive the C tractor that pulls a slip. His job is to ride behind and stack sixty-pound bales of alfalfa into small stacks that we leave at the bottom of the field for later transport to the yard by truck.

We make our way up and down the fields, picking up the bales. I notice he drinks a lot of water and that he spits a lot.

"Hey, kid, can you slow down a little?" he says.

I've been trained to work fast and efficiently. I move the throttle down a few notches, but I don't gear down from second to first. I don't think my father would want me to do that.

Through the heat of the day, we keep pushing ahead. I keep watching him struggle to lift the bales of alfalfa, but I have no compassion for him. I think he's being dramatic and unmanly.

He's too proud to ask me to slow down again. So we just keep going.

Why don't I understand his plight? Why don't I have any empathy for him? Why am I such a cold-hearted manager?

That night, he dies of a heart attack.

*

My parents do their best to keep the news of his death from me. But I eventually learn about it from my mother.

I don't know what to think. I realize the full horror of what happened that day only decades later, when I read Antonio Gramsci's thoughts on cultural hegemony and oppressive structures.

Gramsci would say that I contributed to that man's death by cooperating with a web of ideological values that I did not stop to question. In other words, my culture taught me to be thoughtless, and I was content to be so. I became a cog in a machine that grinds people's lives into sausage, and I gladly played my role.

> then the woman said,
> "Give me that living water"—
> one more dead Indian

At school, I see my friends a bit differently after this incident. Most of my classmates are also sons of farmers. Like me, they work hard. But I doubt they have ever contributed to someone's death like I have.

I wish I could talk with someone about what has happened. But I don't. I can't.

> what lasts after death?
> the nose, the heart, the long bones
> the spirit, the pain?

One day, my sister Annie discovers me crying upstairs in my room.

"What's wrong?" she asks.

"*Everything* is wrong," I answer. "The world is a terrible place."

The Vietnam War is on. People are protesting in the streets. Labor unions are on strike. The Ohio River is flooding. The counterculture is vulgar, but the conservative reaction is cruel and ugly. People like George Wallace are preparing the way for Ronald Reagan, Newt Gingrich, and Donald Trump to move our country toward upheaval.

I see corruption and hypocrisy everywhere I look. In myself, in my teachers at school, in my church leaders, even in my parents. Everyone falls short. I hate the world. I begin to despair. If I sympathize with anyone, it is with the college students in Ohio who get shot down by the National Guard. What did they do to deserve the poisonousness of people blindly following orders?

Annie tells me that I need to "stop thinking so much."

In the years going forward, she will repeat this same advice again and again. My problem is that I think too much. That's who I am, the farm boy who thinks and thinks and thinks until he's stuck in the mud.

I wear bell-bottom pants. My hair is long enough to touch my ears. I play piano and guitar in a band. We're fond of Crosby, Stills, Nash, and Young. But Jimmy Webb's "MacArthur's Park" might be our best number. Our original stuff is written by Robert Skyles, lead guitarist and singer from Mayfield, a tiny town in the foothills to the east.

> *Robert sings—(p)*
> Well, I saw him walk
> walk across the sky.
> He spoke to me
> and I felt high.

We all sing—(ff)
> He was god's poet,
> Yes, he was, the only one.
> Have you seen god's poet?
> Yes, he was, the only one.

One Sunday evening, I go with my family to the seminary building. Lamar Stewart, our stake president, presides over the ordination of my brother Warren to the office of elder in the Melchizedek Priesthood.

Besides being the stake president, Stewart is also my doctor. Every time I go in for a visit, he draws a picture of a smiling guy on my tummy and asks me if I am planning to go on a mission.

I always tell him yes. But do I really want to spend two years of my life knocking on doors?

Doc Stewart asks me to say the opening prayer, and I do. But then I withdraw into my own thoughts. I am no longer scribbling on the walls of the Sigurd chapel. In my mind, I'm typing out the Japanese-American version of John Steinbeck's *The Winter of Our Discontent*.

I keep thinking. That's how I deal with the sorrow. I'm still many years away from learning about *mono no aware*, "the sadness of all things" that Motoori Norinaga proposed as the essence of human existence. I feel the tawdriness of life without relief.

I put up barriers. I retreat into my own world. I even try to shut the gods out, which is the highest foolishness of all. As Nishitani Keiji's correction of Descartes would have it, I think the self exists, therefore I can't help but be miserable and nihilistic.

Thinking doesn't have to make you miserable. Thinking is like exercise. It can make you healthy and strong, or it can lead to injury and decline. It just depends on whether or not you understand certain limitations.

Nishitani was a Kyoto School philosopher. He maintained that the critical force of Western epistemology ultimately, and predictably, led to a harmful kind of nothingness. By comparison, Buddhist skepticism is much deeper and infinitely more thorough. Being so, the deconstructive thought of Nagarjuna and other Mahayana thinkers eventually led to salvation rather than to nihilism. Their nothingness became a fullness rather than a lack.

That said, at this point I am still far from understanding that my pain, and my retreat, are yet another leg of the curving path that leads through sorrow on its way to compassion. A turning away from "The Truth" has to happen if we are to become truly caring as the gods are. But I still don't know this, and so my doubts torture me rather than deliver me from all the pain I am feeling.

In the car, halfway home from the seminary building, I am suddenly struck with a tremendous power. I feel my equilibrium give way. I begin sobbing uncontrollably as the road ahead disappears completely.

We pull up to the house.

My parents have prepared a dinner for Warren. This is his big day. A few of his friends from BYU have come all the way from Provo to celebrate. Everyone gathers downstairs, but I go up to my room to be alone.

The earthquake continues shaking me to the core. I continue to cry for the next two hours.

I can't stop. I can't even stand.

A voice comes to me. "Charles, why do you push me away? Have you forgotten what we promised to do?"

It's exactly as Dwight says. I avoid things. I withdraw from the world.

Guilty as charged.

My aunt Helen, who is also visiting, comes upstairs to comfort me. She puts her arm on my shoulder. She tells me I'm "a good boy," and that I'll be all right. Her arthritic fingers caress my hair. She stays with me for ten minutes, then goes back downstairs to rejoin the party.

I can't stop shaking. Some higher power has knocked me on my back.

I cry for my parents who have to work so hard. I cry for the people dying in Vietnam on both sides of the conflict. I cry for the way Dairy Queen ice cream isn't really ice cream.

But most of all, I cry for myself—for the way I have withdrawn from a world that disappoints me so deeply. I feel a terrible emptiness. Because of my overdeveloped sense of justice—right is right, and wrong is wrong—I've wandered into a fog of sorrow that engulfs and paralyzes me. My insistent search for the truth has landed me in this swamp.

It's not as though I'm a marginal sort of person. I participate in school government. I'm the school photographer, the cocaptain of the wrestling team, the captain of the track team. The women in my school make me the "Most Preferred Man." I'm selected to be a State Star Farmer by the Future Farmers of America Association.

I'm good at welding and geometry. I run the 100-yard dash in 10.7 seconds (on the one day the cheerleaders decided to go to a track meet). I have talent as a dancer, an irrigator, and as a forklift operator.

Strangely, what dancers, irrigators, and forklift operators have in common is a fluid sense of self. This ability to extend one's consciousness into another person, into water, or into a machine is a power that *could* help me escape from my hard shell of self-awareness. This "range" should help me, in the way it obviously helped Joseph Smith and David Bowie. But, as I say, I'm suffering from a tightening sense of ego, which is not helped by the isolation of my rural circumstances. In other words, I'm crippling myself with a growing sense of personal identity, of the maddening sort that the quiet desert winds encourage and adolescence seems to require.

> hear the Buddhists say
> "there's no such thing as the self"—
> sage brush and cedar posts

I later come to understand that what we call "self" is a particularly *modern* concept. The self emerged during the modern era as a "portable sense of home." Identity was once intimately tied to a place—to a particular locale. But as people began to move about, selfhood became a conceptual abstraction that allowed people to inhabit new locations and still remain who they are. Explorers, pioneers, colonists, travelers, and city dwellers all required such a concept in order to inhabit a growing world without suffering a sense of loss.

But there was a price to pay for this convenience. Being cut off from a locale, the self became unbelieving and distanced from the things of its environment. Everything became instrumental, mere objects to be manipulated for our own purposes. Trees became lumber. Clay became bricks. People became labor. God became an "opiate for the masses." Edvard Munch's *The Scream* captures the friendlessness of this ever-moving home-as-self, this—as he put it—"infinite scream passing through nature."

I'm decorating for the FFA Sweetheart Ball. The scaffold on which I am working collapses. I fall twenty feet, and my forehead smacks the floor. Luckily, it's a gym floor that has been designed to have some give to it.

I know I'm still alive. But I can't get up.

I can hear Bobbie Bown running in circles around the tangle of pipes that covers me. He screams, "Charlie's dead! Charlie's dead!"

He pulls the wreckage off, puts me in his pickup truck, and rushes me to the hospital. The bump on my head immediately grows to the size of a baseball.

We speed around a curve, and the door flies open. I almost fall out.

I later teach Bobbie how to go on a date, and he flourishes socially once he gets to Utah State. I tell him, "The secret, Bobbie, is to walk behind the car when you go to open the door for your date."

CHAPTER 5

Father, Nick, Grandfather

My father is frank about sexual matters, but he is a moral man. As a businessman, he occasionally makes what he calls "an honest mistake." Otherwise, he's a man of great integrity.

His explanation for why he is good is simple. "I don't have time to be bad."

It's true. He's either working or sleeping. "I live and breathe farming," he says. For him, life is all about working hard.

He's good at what he does. He tells us to "make winning a habit."

Even though we complain about having to work so hard, we're secretly proud of what we're able to accomplish.

> summer staccato—
> the shop compressor sucks in
> the hot desert air

Capital begins to accumulate. We buy a third farm. We rent two more.

We're irrigating about six hundred acres—none of that with sprinklers and most of it cut up into small sloping fields. That's the hardest kind of farming to do.

My father makes the front cover of *Beet Grower*, *Utah Farmer*, and a few other publications.

"I'm not the smartest person in the world," he often says. "But I make up for what I lack by doubling the effort."

I ask him, "What's the secret to becoming a good farmer?"

His reply surprises me. I'm thinking, "A sense of timing, putting in the hours, etc."

But his answer is "a good farm."

*

And my mother? She works out in the fields too. Then comes home and cooks and cleans. She is often totally exhausted. Yet I never see her collapse on the couch like my father does.

Often too tired to think of what to cook at night, she asks us, "What do you want to eat for dinner?"

*

When my mother met my father at the camp at Heart Mountain, she knew he had graduated from Stanford. Apparently, she thought he would become a lawyer or some other kind of professional who didn't do hard manual labor. She never dreamed he would someday become a farmer. But he did, because of the War.

"Are you sorry you married Daddy?" I ask.

"No," she replies without having to think about it.

My father is temperamental. But because my mother is not, they never fight. Their marriage is as stable as helium. I think it's also because their backgrounds are so similar. They are both children of immigrant Issei farmers. Like my father, my mother is also very intelligent. She was the salutatorian of her class in Toppenish, Washington. After high school, she wanted to study to become a dental assistant, but the men in her extended family (her father died in a car-train accident) forbade it.

My father often tells us, "Don't be harsh." But our circumstances *are* harsh. We live under tremendous economic pressure. By the terms of the agreement my father signed with Newel Childs, if we ever miss even one payment on the farm that we're buying from him, we have to give it back. This was the deal they struck in compensation for the relatively low purchase price that my father negotiated with him. He agreed to pay interest, but on the original amount, not *compounded* interest on the remaining balance.

My father calls the challenge we are up against "stark realism." We know we have to be disciplined. We can't afford to make a mistake, even though farming is one calamity after another—not enough rain, too much rain, late frost, early frost, labor problems, injury, unreliable markets, mechanical failures, and on and on.

Farmers never get the day they planned to have.

Since my family is relatively new to America, we have to work harder than other people. We accept this as a premise of life in a country that was founded on the three realities of hope, slavery, and genocide. This condition of endless work is what makes Americans "great"—if not one's own work, then the work of someone else.

Inouyes are tough. We don't complain, and we certainly don't expect any assistance from a government that rounded us up and put us behind barbed wire. Not expecting help from Uncle Sam makes us strong and independent. But the constant struggle is difficult to bear, especially for my father who often loses his temper when things go wrong. He gets mad at us for not doing things right. Profit margins in farming are razor thin. The possibility of failure is real. We have no guaranteed income, no salary, no rich friends or family to rely on. We face rising costs and falling prices.

I often wonder if city people are aware of how hard country people have to work to provide them with the food they take for granted. Do they know that farmers get 5 cents for the grain in a box of cereal that costs $5?

One day at work, one of our hay-hauling trucks breaks down. I'm trying to weld things back together. My father starts yelling at me for taking too long.

I've had it. I didn't even stop to eat lunch. Why doesn't he appreciate what I do for him?

This time I push back.

"Don't yell at me!" I make a fist and wave it in front of him. "Yell at me one more time, and I'll hit you in the face."

An hour later, he circles back.

He offers his hand in apology. "I'm sorry I provoked you."

We shake hands. "No. I'm sorry. I shouldn't have said that."

We never exchange angry words again. Did I already mention that I love my father?

I am sitting at a long table in Manti, Utah, fifteen miles up the road. It's Thursday evening. I've come to attend the South Sanpete School District Board Meeting with my friend Nick. We're seniors. I'm the student body president of Gunnison Valley High School, and Nick is the drummer in my band. He's in big trouble, and I've come to defend him.

His long hair is in violation of the dress code, and he's about to be expelled.

"You're a good boy," Board Member Wintch says in her charming way. She's the wife of a wealthy cattle rancher in Manti and has a seat at the table.

Nick turns to her. I can tell by the look on his face that he's going to do something stupid. "Don't do it, Nick!" I say to myself.

"You tell me I'm a good boy, Mrs. Wintch," says Nick. "So what's the difference between me now," he reaches up and grabs his wig. "And now?"

He pulls his wig off and his blonde hair cascades to his shoulders.

Holy Batman!—
Abinadi standing before
the wicked priests

Shocked, the superintendent throws himself back into his swivel chair. He smacks the table with his right fist. "By God. We're ready for a lawsuit!" he says. He's tired of fighting noncompliant teenagers and wants the law on his side. "And don't give me any more of that George Washington bullshit."

(We high school students are fond of pointing out that George Washington, Thomas Jefferson, and the other founding fathers of our great nation had long hair. And then there's Jesus. When Jesus comes again, will he have short hair and be wearing a suit and a tie? Anything but cufflinks and JC monographed handkerchiefs, okay?)

rainclouds but no rain—
hippies and Navajos wear
their hair down to here

Mrs. Wintch tries to intervene. "I don't understand it, Nick. You could easily cut your hair. But a black man can't change the color of his skin."

I've been quiet up to this point. But now I explode with anger. "Why would a black person *want* to change the color of his skin?"

I glare at Mrs. Wintch, who is clearly startled by my question.

Can't she see? I'm not white. I'm not like her or anyone else in the room. I never have been. I never will be. Later, when I get to Harvard, I learn how to play squash so I can be the only Asian in a totally white environment.

at Hemenway gym—
I slice the dark rubber ball
into the corner

My irritation reaches a human maximum. Who cares if I upset the others in the room? "Are you crazy?" I shout. "What's wrong with you people?"

"That's it." The superintendent leans forward over the table. He pounds it with his fist again. "We're going to court."

"No, please." Nick's mother finally speaks up. She pleads with everyone to calm down.

*

In the car on the way home, Nick's mother expresses her regrets. "They caught him poaching deer," she says about the superintendent. "I should've said something about *that*."

My father actually had business dealings with the superintendent's father when we were living in Sigurd. He was a good enough guy, I guess. But his son seems like a pretender to me. He later gets a better job and moves away.

*

A week or so later, we hear back from the board about their decision. There's some good news and some bad. Nick can finish high school. He can get a diploma. But he can't attend the graduation ceremony with the rest of us.

"That's garbage." Everyone in my class agrees. We've been through everything together, for as long as we can remember. After years of showering together in the same locker room, are we supposed to be happy with their decision to kick one of us out? We don't want to graduate without Nick there with us.

On graduation day, my commencement address is filled with venom for Cy Andersen. He's the local member of the school board who sits there on the front row. He drives a Cadillac, owns the town bank, owns the showhouse. I have to say that he's not an entirely bad man. As owner of the movie theater, Cy has to babysit for the whole community on Friday nights, patrolling the aisles with his flashlight while everyone's parents are out on the town.

But on graduation day, he represents all that is wrong with the world.

"Why can't we love *everybody*," I preach from my pulpit.

As I talk to an auditorium full of people about the need for love, I feel a burning in my bosom. Is this the beginning of my ministry? Or of my misery?

*

The day before graduation, Nick disappears. Apparently, his mother took him to Las Vegas.

I run into my mother in the kitchen, and she explains. "She didn't want Nick to be in town when the rest of you graduated."

"Really?"

It doesn't occur to me that he would feel so personally hurt by the school board's decision. I doubt he cares, one way or the other. But maybe he does.

That summer, on a warm night in August, just before we go our separate ways, Nick and I ride our bikes to the city park and have a long talk about all the garbage we endured growing up in such a small town.

Those kinds of honest conversations don't happen often. But when they do, you remember them forever. I came to love Nick like a brother. I always will.

> telling the truth
> on a warm summer night—
> the sound of sprinklers

That final summer begins with many dangers for me and my fellow Gunnison Bulldogs. We are like so many hatchery fry, released into a lake filled with big fish and surrounded by anglers with treble hooks and power bait. Kelly Amtoft gets crushed when his jeep rolls over in the White Hills. David Beck loses his military scholarship when the sleeve of his jacket gets caught in a spinning power-take-off shaft. His arm gets broken into many pieces.

Neal Coates. Elaine Yardley. Kelly Mellor. Jenny Christiansen. Since graduation, a number of my classmates have passed on. A part of me dies with them. As I said, we knew everything there was to know about each other.

That was also the summer my grandfather almost passed away. I remember the day clearly.

I'm spraying young barley with 2,4-D. When I get to the bottom of the field, Annie's standing there waiting for me.

"What's up?"

"Quick! It's Grandpa. Come on."

I turn off the engine and jump down to the ground. We push through the reeds canary grass and cross the Dover canal. We get in the car and head for town.

We run into the hospital.

My aunt Ruth is in the room. So is Dillon.

Grandfather is struggling for breath.

Auntie Ruthie has come down from Salt Lake City. She's crying. She is a devout Buddhist, but she asks my brother, "Dillon, can't you do something?"

He nods.

He turns to me. "Charles, can you help me give Grandpa a blessing?"

I shake my head.

"Charles?"

I can't do it. I walk out of the room and head down the hall.

Dillon comes looking for me.

He catches up to me in the lobby.

The morning light pours through the windows. No one is at the front desk, so we're alone. Staring at Bruce Christenson's house across the street, I tell my brother why I can't assist with the blessing. I'm unworthy. I have too many questions and not enough answers.

Gently, Dillon says, "Look. This is not about you. This is about Grandpa. He needs us."

"It wouldn't do any good, coming from me."

"It's not coming from you."

He makes a good point. It's God's blessing to give, not mine. I finally agree.

Together, we walk down the hallway, back to the room. We put our hands on my grandfather's head and give him a blessing. With his usual eloquence, Dillon tells him, "Your time has not yet come. There are things yet to accomplish, lessons to learn."

Immediately, Grandpa's breathing grows smoother. He lives for many more years, until he is ninety-six.

CHAPTER 6

College and a Mission, First Impressions of Japan

MOST OF MY HIGH SCHOOL FRIENDS GO TO UTAH STATE, BUT I decide to attend Brigham Young University. I want to meet people who are smart and believe in god. I need to find a way to deal with how sad the world is.

I get off to an unusual start. Most first-year students live in the dorms, but I share a small rental house with Dwight, Roland Monson, Russell Frandsen, and Dave Hardy. They have all recently returned from their missions.

Because I'm the only first-year student in my ward, my social life is almost nonexistent. The women at BYU don't love you unless you're going on a mission right away or you've just returned from one. I'm neither one nor the other.

Dwight and our three housemates make up for my lack of dating, however. They seek companionship with the earnestness of elk in September. Dwight meets Jeannie Lew from Orem. He admires the way she corrects a vibration in her car by keeping a heavy box of books on the passenger side. She is quiet, and Dwight is quieter still.

I hang out with Kent Mikkelsen, another first-year who is also living off campus with his brother. Kent is a Kimball Scholar, well-educated and faithful. He sings beautifully. He plays handball. He's polite, sophisticated. He's just the kind of person I was hoping to meet.

*

I usually study in the Honors Reading Room. It's a "private" room in the main library where the high achievers hang out. Most of the people there know each other from the Late Summer Honors Program. I couldn't attend because of work on the farm. I feel a little left out. But I like being in the company of talented people.

I notice that every time a certain young woman enters the room, a certain young man gets visibly excited. By the beginning of next term, the two of them are married.

I guess that's how it's supposed to work. The General Authorities often come down from Salt Lake to speak at university-wide devotionals. They tell us that we're getting a big break on tuition and that we should be actively searching for our "eternal companions." That's a fair deal. But, as I said, my viability is pretty low for now.

My top priority lies elsewhere, anyway. I'm desperately trying to survive in an academic environment where everyone else seems much better prepared than I am.

*

I take Introduction to Philosophy from Dennis Rasmussen. He intrigues me. He's the real thing, a true intellectual, a Yale PhD.

He is writing a book, *The Lord's Question*. His argument is simple: Our questions *to* God have been put in our minds *by* God. That being the case, why not ask away?

According to Professor Rasmussen, life should be full of questions and inspired answers. When Enoch sees God weeping over the fate of his children, he asks, "How is it that thou canst weep, seeing thou art holy, and from all eternity to all eternity?" (Moses 7:29).

Even God cries? Are things really that bad? Slowly, I'm beginning to learn that my sadness is nothing when compared to God's sorrow. For that reason alone, it's good to be thankful for the good that happens.

*

Brother Rasmussen takes an interest in me. He invites me to his home for dinner. I meet his wife, Birdie. He has a framed photo of her on the desk in his office. I can tell he is very devoted to her.

He encourages me to study hard. He has the ability to give others hope. Good teachers have this ability. I am forever indebted to him.

*

Of the tens of thousands of students at BYU, I'm usually the last one to leave the library every night.

I'm my father's son. Like him, I, too, think I have to work harder than everyone else just to keep up. Like him, I feel like I'm always behind. No time to go fishing.

> an icy winter night—
> my bicycle slides across
> University Ave

I'm like my father in another way. I also think I'm not that smart. Did I already say that?

*

One day, toward the end the semester, I'm sitting at a table. A typewriter before me. Around me, a stack of books, pens, and crumpled sheets of paper.

Dwight comes by and comments, "You know, you really surprised us." (By "us," he means my three older brothers, who were all better students in high school than I ever dreamed of being.) "We

didn't think you knew how to study. But you're eating this stuff up."
He points to my paper in progress. "Too bad it only lasts for such
a short time."

"What do you mean?"

"Well, you're not going to be writing essays forever, right? Once
college is over, all this . . . ," he looks at my pages of crossed-out
sentences, "is over."

Once again, Dwight's words make a huge impression on me.
The more I think about it, the more I realize I don't want to stop
studying. The truth is, I love writing papers, even more than farming. If I've learned one thing in college, it's that I want to learn how
to think and write well.

I make a trip to Gunnison to tell my parents. I've changed my
mind. I'm not going to take over the farm anymore.

My father is very disappointed. But he says, "Oh, hell. Live
your own life. You have to please yourself."

I often wonder about that evening and about his comment.
After living in the horse stalls at Santa Anita and in the concentration camp at Heart Mountain, was my father able to live *his* own
life? If he did, he survived on the scraps that people like Franklin
Roosevelt, John DeWitt, and Dillon Myer threw to him from their
high table. Why do some people think they can do whatever they
want?

*

Here's the truth about my family situation in the year 1973.
For all their efforts to raise us properly, my parents didn't get the
children they expected. My father, in particular, has a hard time
accepting that we've all become earnest Latter-day Saints.

"You don't need to go on a mission," he tells Dillon and Dwight
and Warren.

But they all do, and he pays their expenses.

He's very Japanese this way. He feels a personal debt (*on*, 恩)
toward his Latter-day Saint neighbors. They give their time and

money to teach and train his children. Not only this, but he also notices that, as long as there is an Inouye on a mission, the flash floods that regularly rush down Hayes Canyon stop coming.

By his own admission, he's not a man of faith. Speaking of our Latter-day Saint neighbors, he often says, "I don't have what they have."

Just the same, he begins to wonder if god exists and if it's possible to be blessed. Do the gods prevent flash floods? Can the gods help a family like ours pay their debts and eventually prosper?

After three semesters at BYU, I feel confident enough in my faith to put in an application to go on a mission. A month later, I am called to the Japan Sapporo Mission. I sign the letter and send it back to Salt Lake City. I promise to dedicate myself to the service of others. To show my sincerity, I give up dancing and hunting.

February 1974. The day to leave home comes around. I don't ask my mother for one last haircut. Haircutting time was when we talked privately about the things on my mind. I'm afraid I would cry if we had a conversation now. So I say no to the offer. Slowly but surely, I'm learning to appreciate my mother for all the things I assumed all mothers just do.

Turning down the offer to "look presentable," I just show up at the mission home, long-haired and darkly tanned from working outdoors with Henry. We've been cutting down cottonwood trees at the Childs farm. My father hates the moaning of the wind as it rushes through the branches. He calls it "the sound of hell."

Sitting down with all the other new missionaries, I immediately get pulled from the crowd and sent to a nearby barber.

I walk in the door and say, "I'm a missionary."

He nods. Without bothering to ask, he has at it. He's obviously been in this situation before. Soon, my long black hair covers his linoleum floor.

leaving the world—
the barber's daughter is
serving in Madrid

Back in my seat, my hair cropped short, I'm as eager as Saigyō to begin a new life. I listen to many talks about the need to be cleansed from the stains of the world. I feel the desire to repent. I confess my sins to a very understanding man who tells me, "Some of us were noticing your nice smile." He declares me forgiven and thanks me for coming to talk with him. He wishes me the best. Purged of iniquity, I am more eager than ever to serve with "heart, might, mind, and strength" (Doctrine and Covenants 4:2).

*

We fly from Salt Lake City to Honolulu, Hawaii. We take a bus to Laie, where we're going to spend the next two months learning Japanese. I am called to be the zone leader of our group of about sixty people.

a first test of faith—
the steepness of the mountains
is hard to believe

We settle into a strict routine—classes all morning and review sessions in the afternoon and evening. We get an hour a day for exercise and take breaks for meals.

I experience something like the gift of tongues. It's not that I wake up one morning speaking Nihongo. But I do make unusually quick progress learning a language that is the trunk of one of the tallest and most heralded trees in the forest.

Generally speaking, Latter-day Saint missionaries are good at learning languages. Not everyone becomes a "language giant." But we all get to where we can teach the rudiments of the gospel. It's kind of miraculous, when you think about it.

Our vocabulary is a bit odd, I have to admit. We can say, "After baptism, you will receive the gift of the Holy Ghost." But we don't know how to say, "Where's the bathroom?"

It is the last week in February. The weather is pleasant. I walk to Laie Point with Jones-chōrō, my companion. He's a skinny, pleasant guy from Idaho. We stand on the ancient flow of lava that has run out into the sea and hardened. I am awed by the thirty-foot waves that come crashing in. We actually saw the surf from the plane as we approached the island. The massive waves were lined up like the rows of a washboard.

> white shirts and dark ties—
> Jesus turns the massive surf
> into a sandy beach

Evening devotionals consist of an opening song, two prayers, and a talk. One of the speakers, I think his name was Brother Honda, gives the same speech three times in two months. Each time he does, he repeats the same passage of scripture over and over.

> And the Lord called his people Zion, because they were of one heart and one mind, and dwelt in righteousness; and there was no poor among them. (Moses 7:18)

"What is Zion?" I wonder. "And why does this guy think it's so important?"

> horn-rimmed glasses—
> Brother Honda once again
> Zion this and that

I start thinking seriously about Brother Honda's talks. What does "no poor among them" mean exactly? And how is the "one heart and one mind" of Zion accomplished? When I later visit Cuba and (precapitalist) China, I think of these words and feel strangely at home among the communists.

Latter-day Saint society, like the Inouye family, is built on socialist principles. In our business dealings with the world, we are capitalists *par excellence*. But in our interactions with each other, we believe that everything belongs to God and that we are merely caretakers of his vineyard. According to Brother Honda, the true sign of a society's righteousness is how well it takes care of the poor.

Who was it that said, "Take what you need, and give the rest to others"?

> the hands that hang down—
> my stake president drives a
> a black BMW

One night during study break, I try the vending machine.

> a cool evening breeze—
> in go three quarters and
> out comes a rat

For the first time in my life, I am truly happy. Never has my mind been so focused. By the time I leave for Japan, I have memorized the entire lesson plan. Without knowing what all the words mean, I've locked a hundred or so pages of text into perfect order. My teachers tell me they don't think anyone's ever done that before.

Once again, I don't mention this to boast, but only to note once again how much you can accomplish when the Spirit is energizing you.

On the plane from Honolulu to Tokyo, I see my first Japanese movie. Directed by Yamada Yōji, *It's Hard to Be a Man* is thoroughly puzzling. I can't understand why it's even a movie. There's not much of a plot, and the characters are not well developed.

Many years later, I become addicted to Yamada's Tora-san films. I watch all forty-eight of them, some as many as ten times. I also come to appreciate his gentler, kinder samurai trilogy—*Twilight Samurai*, *The Hidden Blade*, and *Love and Honor*. At this point, though, as the plane descends toward Tokyo, Japanese culture is a huge puzzle to me.

*

We have a brief layover at Haneda Airport. I am standing on the second floor, looking down on an open atrium. Everything is white marble—the walls, the columns, the floor. I watch numbers of young Japanese women pulling their suitcases across that smooth, bright surface.

Someone has just come up with the idea to put wheels on suitcases. The invention of the pull-up handle is still ten years away. All you had back then was a short leather thong, like a dog leash, that you attached to your bag.

As I look down at those women coaxing their luggage across the white expanse, I exclaim under my breath, "They're beautiful!"

They are dressed in tailored wool suits. The delicate and attentive way they trail their suitcases behind them impresses me greatly.

*

On the connecting flight to Sapporo, as I settle into my seat, I begin to wonder. Why should I be surprised that Japanese women are attractive?

I generate two possible explanations.

- Explanation one. The few Japanese women I know are all my relatives. An incest taboo has kept me from considering them alluring.
- Explanation two. Only *white* women are supposed to be beautiful. I've imbibed a form of self-loathing from my cultural

environment. As a member of a racial minority, I accept my ugliness as an obvious truth.

Whichever the reason, this discovery of people who look like me is emancipating. By the time the plane lands at Chitose Airport, I've resolved to master the Japanese language and learn all I can about Japanese culture. I already sense that if I learn what I can about my cultural heritage, I'll be better able to tolerate life in the United States.

I guess I'm slowly learning my need to be saved—not only from sin, but from American racism, from capitalism, from male chauvinism, from classism, from Cocoa Puffs, and from much, much more.

CHAPTER 7

The Work,
Many Are Chilled

THERE'S NOTHING EASY ABOUT BEING A MISSIONARY. MY FIRST evening on the job, we visit a fishing village near the port city of Otaru. I'm standing at the opened door of a fisherman's shack. I begin to deliver my newly memorized approach. "We represent The Church of Jesus Christ of Latter-day Saints."

The man has a hole in his throat. The white towel that hangs over it flares out every time he tries to talk. I can't understand what he's trying to say. But judging from the look in his eyes, and from the violent dancing of his towel, I think he's telling me to get lost.

Wow, missionary life is even more difficult than farming. Most of our days are spent in a near futile search for investigators. We go from house to house, trying to find someone who is waiting to be taught the gospel. To borrow an idiom from Mencius, it's a little like searching trees for fish.

We employ three different strategies:

1. *The meaning-of-life approach.* "We represent The Church of Jesus Christ of Latter-day Saints. We have a slide show called *Man's Search for Happiness.* We'd like to show it to you."
2. *The importance-of-the-family approach.* "We represent The Church of Jesus Christ of Latter-day Saints. We'd like to introduce you to family home evening, a program designed to strengthen ties between family members."

If neither of these works, there's always number three.

3. *The give-me-your-bicycle approach.* "We represent The Church of Jesus Christ of Latter-day Saints. Can we have that bicycle you left out in the snow all winter?"

A surprising number of people leave their bikes outside in the cold weather. By the time the snow melts, they're pretty much unusable.

We learn how to put four or five rusty bicycles together to make one good one. Unusable parts are scattered all over the ground in front of our apartment. The pile of bike carcasses grows higher by the day. We consider putting up a sign that reads "Latter-Day Bicycle," 末日自転車.

> the neighbors complain—
> Mormon elders drag race
> on a narrow street

I am standing in an arcade, a few flyers in hand, trying to get up enough nerve to approach one of the people passing by.

"You know," I say to myself, "you're not very good at this."

"You know," I say to myself, "if people are walking on a street, it's usually because they're trying to get somewhere else."

"You know," I say to myself, "if this is what a mission is all about, two years is going to be a very long time."

Above our heads are speakers from which pour jingles for ramen and eyeglasses. They get played on the public PA system over and over. They're driving me mad.

＊

"Ramen, ramen-ya. Mittsu." ("Ramen, Mr. Ramen. Gimme three.")

"Megane no koto nara, Megane no Fuji." ("If you're thinking of glasses, it's Fuji Glasses.")

Thank goodness for P-day (preparation day), when we can take a break from our usual schedule. I am with Shepherd-chōrō, Black-chōrō, and Hirano-chōrō. We decide to go see the ocean. We end up in a small cove surrounded by steep cliffs. The beach is stony. We watch the sun set. It envelops us in a golden light, the color of molten copper. The lines between the sky, sea, cliffs, and beach all blur in a profusion of sunlight. For the first time, I feel the beauty of the sublime.

> a beach of round stones—
> a fishing boat disappears
> into nothingness

I get transferred to Sapporo, the capital city of Hokkaido. Miracles begin to happen. A woman who has lost her hearing comes to the Sapporo chapel with a friend. The friend tells us the woman wants to be healed. At first I hesitate. But then I remember. My patriarchal blessing says that I will "heal the sick." And didn't my grandfather get better after the blessing Dillon and I gave him?

We anoint her head and give her a blessing. The next day, she comes back alone to thank us. Her hearing has been completely restored. I'm surprised, but she is not.

＊

We come up with ways to keep things interesting. We devise a game to play while house-to-housing. Just before a door opens, you give your companion a word. It can be any word, but it has to be used in the approach.

For example, "miso soup."

*

"Good morning. We represent The Church of Jesus Christ of Latter-day Saints. If you have a minute, we'd like to talk with you about miso soup and our purpose here on earth."

*

Japanese people find it remarkable that non-Japanese can say even the most basic things in their language. Maybe for that reason, our word games go practically unnoticed. There might be three degrees of glory in the afterlife, but I quickly learn that in this life there are at least a thousand degrees of weird.

As a Japanese-looking person who can't speak Japanese, I provide one of those degrees of weirdness. My companion Shephard-chōrō speaks Nihongo a hundred times better than I. Still, when he asks a question, the people look at me and give their answer.

When I can't answer back, they don't know where to look.

No one said it was going to be easy. Finding investigators is made even harder by a mandate from President Koizumi, architect and military man from Honolulu. He wants us to teach families rather than individuals since salvation is a family matter.

That's doctrinally correct. No argument there. But as a practical matter, it's much easier to teach college students who have the time and freedom to take the lessons. They can always make families later, no?

*

The days pass slowly. At times I want to speak with the trump of angels. But the big lesson I'm slowly learning is that there's nothing efficient (or modern) about a god who leaves the ninety-nine to go after the one. We have little success. Morale is not great. President Koizumi gets mad at me for writing in my weekly report, "We're not having much luck."

"It's not about luck, Inouye-chōrō. It's about faith."

＊

We keep ourselves alive on the cracked wheat we buy at a chicken feed store. We also eat the ends of loaves (*pan no mimi*) that the bread factory usually throws away. We buy them by the bagful, swept up off the floor.

A high point of my week is divvying up this discarded bread. There are always two or three nice, thick slices in every bag.

It's very cold. The wind blows right through my Harris Tweed coat. I am discouraged. I miss my family. The snow starts falling on the first of November and doesn't melt off until the rains of Easter.

＊

I get transferred to Asahikawa. The snow is even deeper, the air colder. I've never heard so many barking dogs. Half of them are named Shiro (Whitey)—a name not so different from Shirō (Fourth Son), my middle name. The only difference is the extended vowel. Two counts for *ō*, and one for *o*. Extended vowels are one of the hardest things about Japanese for me to master.

＊

I am peddling down a street. Tires scream, and WHAM!

Suddenly, I am flying through the air. I land twenty feet away, on the side of the road.

The driver, a young man in his thirties, runs over to where I'm lying in the weeds.

He and my companion help me up. I walk around. To everyone's surprise, including mine, I'm not seriously injured. All those years of loading semitrailers with hundred-pound sacks of potatoes are paying off.

My body is strong. I'm fine. But the man's car is ruined. There's a gaping hole in the front grill. The antenna is smashed so it conforms perfectly to both the hood and windshield. The glass is shattered all the way across.

Once again—for the third or fourth time?—my life has been spared.

How many "escape death" cards are in my deck?

*

I get transferred to Muroran. It's a blue-collar, ship-building town with a reputation for being a hard place to do the Lord's work. For me, though, the gritty streets feel a little like home.

In the ocean we baptize one of our investigators.

> seagulls and the spirit—
> God makes the green ocean waves
> gently rise and fall

We find and begin teaching the Abo family. They eventually get baptized.

*

We are house-to-housing in the west part of town. Suddenly, my companion, Otsue-chōrō, tells me we need to go back to the apartment.

"What's wrong?"

"I have to use the bathroom."

"We just got here. Can't we find a public toilet somewhere?"

I know what he'll say. Otsue likes things to be clean. He once got upset with me for sitting on his pillow.

"We have to go back," he insists.

"All right. If you say so."

We catch the next bus home. There's a lot of traffic for some reason. We make slow progress.

Otsue is stone-faced. I can tell he's really nervous about how slow the bus is going.

At last, we finally get to our stop. As soon as the door opens, Otsue takes off. Missionaries are supposed to stay with their companions at all times, but he's nowhere in sight. I'm feeling lonely walking by myself through the narrow streets of Muroran. It's been a year since I walked anywhere alone.

I get to our apartment and start climbing the flight of steel steps. I open the door. The washing machine is running.

"I shouldn't have run," Otsue says.

*

We teach a single man named Konishi. He's a good-natured, rotund fellow in his forties. He ekes out a living by doing laundry. His home is filled with clothes hanging out to dry. He heats his house with a simple coal-burning stove. At some point in the past, the fire had gotten so hot that the steel had melted, leaving the stove misshapen, pulled down by gravity, *à la* Oldenburg.

We learn that Konishi eats only boiled eggs and small hard biscuits that he buys in big thirty-pound bags. Whenever we visit, he prepares this simple meal for us.

It's a joy to teach him. He loves to sing the hymns and to hear about Jesus's Atonement. "The gift of resurrection and the possibility of redemption from sin is given to everyone," we teach him. I myself am just beginning to understand why salvation is a gift and not something that we earn.

*

As I write this, I'm filled with memories of walking down the narrow streets of Muroran with Konishi. Everyone we meet greets him as if he were Hotei, the beloved laughing monk. After a month or so, I get transferred back to Sapporo to work in the mission home. Fortunately, my new job comes with a lot of traveling. We visit Muroran a few months later for a zone conference, and Konishi shows up on his scooter. He hands me a brown paper sack, gives me a warm smile and a handshake.

On the train back to the city, I open the bag. It's filled with hard-boiled eggs and biscuits.

The work is hard. But, on the other hand, we "elders of Israel" achieve a kind of humility that is rare in twenty-year-olds. Raking

24/7 helps you find joy in the smallest things. While making dinner one evening, we come up with an ode to *yakisoba* (fried noodles).

To be sung to the tune of "Oklahoma."

> *Yakisoba* instant gastronomical delight.
> To fix they're quick
> But they'll make you sick
> If you eat one almost every night.
> Food value you know they ain't got.
> And if you eat 'em, your stomach'll rot.
> So when we saaay, "*YAKisoba*'s on the waaay."
> We're only saying
> "You're frying fine *yakisoba*
> *Yakisoba*, Y-A-K-I-S-O-B-A
> *YakisooBA!*"

The Japan Sapporo Mission covers the northern island of Hokkaido, from Hakodate in the south to Wakkanai in the north. It's terribly cold. We take our motto—"Many are chilled but few are frozen—from Matthew 22:14: "Many are called but few are chosen."

✻

Something unexpected happens. Our prophet, Spencer W. Kimball, visits us. He has come for a conference with the saints in Japan. On his way back to the United States from Tokyo, he makes a stop in Hokkaido, probably because one of us, Mack-chōrō, is his grandson.

I'm working in the mission home, so I get to interact closely with President Kimball. During our all-mission conference, I sit next to him on the stand and interpret. I can feel his holiness. Compared to the other people in his entourage—including his personal physician and secretary—he is far more spiritually accomplished.

I can tell he's a sanctified man. He's full of love. He's humble. Meeting him, I relax a little. I realize that it's going to take a lifetime of raking to become anything like him. That kind of purity of heart is not something you can accomplish overnight.

It also occurs to me, for the first time, that people *can* become perfected. Sure, it's difficult. But as long as one person has gotten there, the rest of us don't have an excuse for not trying.

I later read his essay "The False Gods We Worship" (*Ensign*, June 1976) and see why he is such a profoundly good man. Has a prophet of God ever written such moving words, connecting compassion with our relationship to the earth?

＊

Fall comes, then winter. Working in the heated mission office, I miss the transition from warm to cold weather. President Koizumi, a man I've grown to love and respect, sends me to Obihiro for my last two months.

The temperature never climbs above zero. I'm so cold my bones ache. Going from house to house, I wonder if I'm ever going to be warm again. Back at the apartment, we put our eggs in the refrigerator to keep them from freezing.

＊

I develop a cough. I'm physically exhausted.

Still, I don't want to go home. I can't even imagine what life after my mission will be like.

A month later, my two years are over. The plane climbs away from Tokyo, and Mt. Fuji disappears in the distance. I finally break down in tears.

Who can possibly understand what I have just been through? The trials, the loneliness, the cold, the hunger, the miracles, the blessings, the lessons learned from raking day after day. People make fun of Latter-day Saint missionaries. But if they took the time to listen to what they have to say, they would learn something astonishing and important—not because the missionaries know all the answers but because they are "true messengers" of god.

> in my first-class seat—
> the stewardess offers me
> wine but no bread

CHAPTER 8

Henry, and Despair

WHEN I WAKE UP, I'M IN HAWAII. IT'S WARM. THE AIR SMELLS like flowers. The sky is bright.

My mother has come as far as Honolulu to meet me. It's great to see her again. We spend a week visiting relatives, including a long-lost cousin who lets me drive his motorcycle up and down his street in the Honolulu suburbs.

We fly back to Los Angeles, then drive north to Palo Alto to say hello to Dillon, who is getting his PhD in psychology at Stanford.

A day later, we finally get back to good ol' Gunnison. My parents have moved to a small two-bedroom house in the country. They left town to be in closer proximity to my grandfather during his final months. He died while I was in Japan, so I missed the funeral.

I feel his absence. The fluorescent lights glare on the linoleum floor. When I meet my father, he seems diminished by the loss of his father.

*

My mother prepares a homecoming meal. It's just the three of us. While we're eating, the phone rings. The Mexican workers are calling from a payphone at the Wisteria Café in town.

I piece together the conversation. Henry Timican, the Paiute man who has been working for my father for as long as I can remember, is drunk. I realize that, for the two years of my mission, I have forgotten about him completely.

He has a gun. The Mexicans are afraid he's going to shoot them.

My father insists I stay home and rest. But I put on a coat and go with him to check up on Henry. I've seen him in his drunken rage many times. Before my mission, I even wondered if he might murder my father someday.

> gunshots in the valley—
> a pheasant tumbles head first
> into the salt grass

As we ride in silence to the Childs farm, I remember going with my mother once to bail Henry out of jail. Reed Blomquist, justice of the peace, takes me aside. "Young man, don't judge Henry. He's the way he is because the people in this community hate him and his people. That's why he drinks like he does."

When Henry is sober, he's a gentleman. When drunk, he's filled with rage. He used to come to the house and argue with my father. As I said, I actually wondered if, one sad day, he would kill my father in anger.

*

We find Henry in his room. We turn on the light.

He's lying on a mattress that glistens with spittle.

My father voices his displeasure. "Why do you have a gun?"

Henry props himself up on an elbow. He yells back in a slurred voice. "To protect *you*, Charlie. If I didn't have a pistol, those white boys would steal you blind." By "white boys," he means the local hoodlums who siphon gasoline out of farm trucks and tractors. It happens all the time.

While they talk, I walk around the room. The top drawer of Henry's desk is open. I see his pistol and a box of bullets.

I also notice that Henry's two-burner cookstove is hissing propane. I click the knob to off.

On the drive back home, the night engulfs us. Behind us, our taillights catch a long, red contrail of dust that hangs frozen in the winter air. I haven't seen this many stars for two years.

> above the mountain's edge
> ten billion stars scream—
> "You forgot Henry!"

I finally mention the stove to my father. "With the windows covered over with plastic like that, he would have died for sure."

My father's reaction surprises me. "Don't think you can save Henry," he says, almost angrily. "There's nothing you can do. That's none of your business."

*

By the time we get back to the house, I understand how completely I have forgotten about this man who was once such a big part of my life. We worked side by side for all those years. We shared a life together. But then I left for my mission, and he vanished from my mind completely.

Missionaries are told to forget the world, to focus on the work at hand. But did I go too far in my need to please god? I begin to wonder if my search for purity was just another excuse to separate myself from other people. I am reminded of my weakness and realize I am not fixed. Not at all. The thought makes me very sad.

As I walk into the house, it dawns on me. "I've missed the whole point of my mission." What lack I yet? In trying to reach perfection by obeying all the rules and working hard to stay clean, I've been going the wrong direction—not *into* life but *away* from it.

In two years, I've made myself into a pure crystal ball, beautifully disciplined and accomplished. But now I can see that I was trying for the wrong kind of beauty. I've been following the admonition of Saul, not of Paul.

> don't tolerate sin!
> holding the robes of the
> stone throwers

I remember. There was this man in Sapporo. He was married to one of our investigators. In response to President Koizumi's instructions to teach families rather than individuals, Elder Buchanan and I kept asking if her husband could join our discussions. One day, he suddenly shows up.

At the end of the lesson, we turn to him. "So what do you think about the things we've been teaching your wife?"

Without hesitating, he says, "If I thought you cared the slightest about me, I might listen to what you have to say. But it's obvious you don't."

The words sting because they are true.

In fact, I don't really care about the details of his life. I just want him to take the lessons with his wife because those are the rules. That's our goal: to teach and baptize as many families as we can.

What a miserable failure I am! In my wish to be a good missionary, did I ever stop to think about what my obedience was supposed to accomplish? All this time, raking without knowing why.

I feel my soul shatter into a million pieces. I realize I'm going to have to start all over. Suddenly, I'm a million shards on the ground. Maybe I'll put myself together. But this time I'll have to use glue of every possible color.

Summer drags on. Charles is miserable. He's not just unhappy. He's depressed. There's something physically wrong with him as well. He starts getting boils all over his body. He catches a virus and ends up in the hospital.

Life becomes terribly out of balance. Something is missing. Nothing motivates me. None of my goals mean anything anymore. I realize that I have misunderstood god, that I've used up all my energy for the wrong reasons. I was given a golden opportunity, but I blew it. I realize I have nothing to live for.

A few bad days become a few bad weeks. The Spirit leaves me. I am truly alone. I'm horrified to realize I don't believe in anything anymore. It's that simple.

All the things I learned on my mission mean nothing to me now. All the miracles, all the blessings.

I finally understand what hopelessness feels like.

The silence of the Utah countryside moves in. Self-pity takes over. The crew of devils who are assigned to me sense an opportunity. "Look at that. Prince Charles has finally worn himself out."

The days drag on. They persuade me to end it all. "Why not? What's the point of your meaningless life? What did you think you were going to accomplish, anyway?"

I have nothing to say in response.

They're right. Everything is horribly sad. Everything is disappointing. There's really nothing to salvage of the wreck that I've so quickly become. I'm totaled, not worth fixing. Hasn't my homecoming proven that? I've not only missed the point of my mission. I've missed the point of my life.

I search for and find my shotgun. It's in the back of the closet, next to a metal file box.

I decide to open the box. My parents gave it to me for Christmas when I was a senior in high school. I thought it was an unusual

zion earth zen sky

gift at the time, though I now understand why my parents wanted me to start keeping a record of my life.

A high school diploma. A few medals and ribbons. A couple of photos and newspaper clippings.

I examine everything. Normally, these mementoes would have given me some sense of accomplishment. But I've come to them a little too late. It's as if they belong to someone I used to know, not to me. That past version of me might have been a real fool, a true *baka*. But at least he had faith.

I pull my shotgun out of its case. I find a shell and push it into the magazine. I lock the round into the firing chamber. I sit on the edge of my bed and take off my shoes.

I click off the safety. I put the barrel to my mouth.

I'm in a trance. I feel the trigger with my big toe. I am about to tap it and blow my head off, when I have a thought.

"Look." The Spirit finally breaks through my shell of self-pity. It raises a last-minute question that saves me. "How sad will your mother and father be if you kill yourself? Can you do that to them? Are you really *that* ungrateful and selfish?"

I put the gun down and eject the shell from the chamber.

No. I am not that selfish.

> "What am I doing?"—
> a brass and plastic shotgun shell
> rolls on the carpet

That was a close call. I'm still alive. But I'm desperate. I need to do something. But what?

86

CHAPTER 9

California

OVER THE NEXT FEW DAYS, I DECIDE THAT IF I'M GOING TO FIX what's wrong with me—if I'm to heal my deep contempt for the world—I need to get out of Utah. Ironically, I'm losing my faith not because I'm too worldly but because I'm not worldly *enough*.

No rich and poor? How can I make Zion happen if I don't know who the rich and the poor are?

*

I'm pretty confused. But one thing is obvious. I can't go back to BYU. The wide sidewalks and the carefully clipped lawns are comforting. The students are wholesome and intelligent. But my path has to take me into the wilderness, not away from it.

Siddhartha left the palace. Adam and Eve left the garden. Abraham left Ur. I need to leave Utah. I need to live on the other side of the Zion Curtain long enough to learn what the world really is, and what my relationship to it should be.

The odds are not good, but I put in an application to transfer to Stanford. My approach is short and direct. I say a few things about wanting to study Japanese literature with Makoto Ueda, but then I get to the real point. "I need to get out here," I write. "Help! Get me out of Utah!"

*

A couple of months later, I come in from the fields to find a thick envelope on the kitchen table. To my surprise, Stanford wants me. My father is upset that I didn't consult with him before applying. Palo Alto is going to be a lot more expensive than Provo.

In the end, though, he comes up with the tuition check. He knows he owes me this one indulgence. I know it too. I have been faithful to him since day one. I have worked my heart out for him.

This is something I have to do. I'm in crisis. He, of all people, understands that. My life is hanging in the balance.

*

Fall comes. I leave home. When I get to northern California, I'm surprised to find that it feels familiar. In fact, I feel more at home here than anywhere I've ever been before, Japan included. Maybe it's because my father used to live in the Bay Area. In a sense, this is where we Inouyes are from. We're essentially Californians transplanted to Utah.

My grandparents once farmed small plots of land in Sunnyvale, Mountain View, Menlo Park, and Redwood City. They grew a few acres of strawberries and raspberries here and there, even on Stanford campus in Palo Alto.

The oat-covered hills dotted with live oak are my new home, and I'm excited to be back where my family once lived.

*

I settle in. I major in Japanese. I study with Professor Ueda, a scholar who does research on both early-modern and modern Japanese literature. All my mentors will follow this same pattern of studying both periods, as will I.

I study hard. I continue to get good grades.

＊

Utah fades away. But the tie is always there. A few months later, the phone in my dorm room rings. It's my mother. "We just wanted to let you know that Henry passed away."

In my mind, I see the half-healed knife scars on Henry's arms. The day before I left for Palo Alto, he rolled up his sleeves and showed me his wounds. He was starting to get into fights. I knew then that he didn't have much time left. But I didn't think the end would come so soon.

> almost late for class—
> I cry for Henry and for
> Akutagawa

When classes are over in the spring, I get a ride back to Utah and start working on the farm again. One day in late June, the hydraulics on the Massey-Ferguson fail. I make a trip to Richfield to get parts.

Where the main road turns left, I turn right. I drive past the park to the Paiute Canal. I take another right. I turn into the circle of unpainted houses and mobile homes that is the Indian village.

It is mercilessly hot. The sunlight feels like acid on my forearms. A dog with porcupine quills festering in its nose comes up to me. I find Henry's nephew Bobby sitting on a chair outside one of the houses. He invites me in.

We sit at the kitchen table, and he tells me what happened.

"We came back from Koosharem that night. We was drinking, you know. So when Henry had a heart attack, by the time them medics showed up, it was too late. His lips was purple."

Bobby offers me a glass of water from the sink.

He sits back down at the table. "Henry was a great hunter. He always got his deer."

"I didn't know he hunted."

"Yeah. He was a great shot. Never missed."

I think to myself, "So it wasn't suicide, at least not with a gun."

"The funeral was real nice. Your dad gave a talk. There was flowers and everything."

We continue chatting, and I learn from Bobby an astonishing fact about Henry. He was the chief of his tribe. This man who drove tractor for my father for so many years was king of the Southern Paiutes.

Hearing this, I feel the sadness of the world more strongly than ever. Henry was a king, but to the people of Richfield he was nothing but a drunkard.

The pioneers who settled "the valleys of the mountains" took the Paiute land and made it their own. They disrupted their way of life and insulted their pride. Then, as if that weren't enough, they sold Henry the alcohol that finally destroyed him and his family. To be fair, very few people in town actually had any direct dealings with him and his people. But that was precisely the problem. Their indifference and contempt was the reality of Henry's life.

In the fall, I return to Stanford. The eucalyptus groves of northern California welcome me back. This time the palm trees leading to campus greet me with warmth and excitement. This is where I belong.

I live on the third floor of a mansion in the old part of Palo Alto. My roommate is Scott Lambert, also a returned missionary. We share a room. The owners are going through a divorce, and we are there to pay rent and to help everybody feel a little less vulnerable.

Scott is one of the nicest people I've ever met. He's premed and studies a lot. He later becomes a famous eye surgeon and a member of the Stanford Medical School faculty.

I am excited to be learning so much. But my desire to know the world is starting to wear on me. I understand that I am useless to God without the knowledge I'm gaining. But I also quickly realize that it isn't easy to learn about the world without becoming worldly.

As I understand more about other ways of thinking, and as my ability to reason becomes sharper, I come to see just how narrow my life has been up to this point. I start to dismiss the things I once believed to be accidents of history rather than gifts from the gods. In an effort to take stock of what I can and can't trust, I form the opinion that honesty and integrity are what matter most. That being the case, I decide to jettison anything I'm not completely sure of. By definition, that would have to include everything having to do with faith.

As the new school year begins, my willingness to live worshipfully grows steadily weaker. By December, I don't feel comfortable at church anymore. I begin to wonder about other possibilities.

By April, exhausted by weeks and months of internal debate, I finally decide to call it quits. I know I will miss the sugar cookies. But leaving is the honest thing to do. I have to try too hard to be a member of The Church of Jesus Christ of Latter-day Saints.

*

I decide to attend sacrament meeting at the Stanford Ward one last time. I sing the hymns one last time. I take the sacrament one last time. I hear the prayers one last time. It's not that I don't appreciate all the things I've learned as a member. It's not that I don't need the cheerfulness of the community. And it's not that I've forgotten all the blessings that have come my way.

It's just that I've come to see other ways, more *honest* and less chauvinistic ways, of being in the world.

When the meeting is over, I try to leave the chapel as quickly as possible. I slide to the end of the pew, ready to make my getaway.

But there's a problem. My friend Dale Nielsen is standing there in the aisle.

I first met Dale at BYU, on the set of a television program in which Professor Rasmussen delivered a lecture to a few students. He's since become a physics student at Stanford. I've come to respect him as the elders quorum president and as my home teacher. He is a sincere and faithful man.

He senses something's up. "Are you okay?"

I tell him I'm fine. But he knows I'm hurting.

"Hey, if there's anything I can do to help, just let me know."

The thing about Dale is that when he says "if there's anything I can do to help," he really means it. He is earnest and true in the way faithful Latter-day Saints are. For a brief moment, I remember all the good people I grew up with in Sigurd and Gunnison, the people I met at BYU, and the people I taught on my mission.

But I tell myself not to be sentimental. "Come on. Get out of here!"

The aisle in the chapel is crowded with people visiting with each other. I push my way through and finally make it to the back of the room.

As I turn toward the exit, Patricia Webb jumps up from the pew that lines the back wall. She's going to Stanford, too, getting her master's degree in education. She stands in front of me. She blocks my way.

With tears in her eyes, she asks, "Charles, when are you going to visit me? Have you forgotten me?"

I am *her* home teacher. And, yes, I have forgotten her. In my self-absorption, I've let my duties slip. I think, "Sorry, Patty. You're on your own now." But how can I actually say that to her?

I awkwardly step to the right and continue on.

I push through the exit and step outside. Finally, I've escaped! No more raking for me.

I make my way to the parking lot. The air is clear. The sun is bright.

Everyone inside the building now belongs to my past. I am free to leave the gravitational pull of all religions, once and for all. I have a new secular future, one more honest and realistic. I feel courageous. I feel good about what I've just done. But suddenly my feet come to a stop.

"What just happened?"

A voice in my head launches a string of questions. They come at me like bullets from an automatic rifle. "You decided to end your life of faith. But then what happened? First, you met your home teacher. He offered to help you. Then you met your home teachee. She asked for your help.

"One person was there to care for you. The other was there to be cared for by you.

"And your response?

"Like Jonah, you ran away!

"Is that who you are—the farm boy who still runs away from people? Is this what your newly found honesty gets you?"

The voice stops being my own at some point and starts being someone else's. I've heard the voice once before, on the night of my brother Warren's ordination.

"Look, Charles. Think about what you know, not about what you don't know. Keep the focus on loving others, and someday you'll have all the answers you need. I promise. Until you truly learn to care for others, you'll never be the person you want to be."

What gentle instruction! Were I not walking in a quiet garden, I probably would not have heard his words. But I do. For the second time, Jesus's voice speaks directly to my heart.

By the time I get to my pickup in the parking lot, I change the course of my life—once again.

I go back to church that next Sunday. I've been going back ever since.

In our search for enlightenment, we face *two* points of conversion. The first is a turning away from the burning house—the world of illusion that captures us. When we leave it behind and begin our climb toward the truth, we enter the realm of justice. We learn the difference between right and wrong. We learn how to choose the right.

We are encouraged at first. It feels good to be right and just. But gradually we realize that the justice we seek brings sorrow rather than happiness. A world that is fair, where everyone gets what they deserve, is *not* what we want. This is surprising, not at all what we expected. In the fog of pain that our searching inevitably brings, we are given the chance to see justice differently and to turn again. This time, we turn away from justice-as-truth, away from what we thought was our ideal reality.

If we simply refuse to move ahead, to push through the fog of sorrow that obscures the way ahead, we remain trapped in the realm of justice. Eventually, we become judgmental, cynical, proud, bitter. But if our rebellion causes us to keep moving forward, even as we turn away, then we eventually enter the path of compassion-as-truth, the reality that is meant to be. It is a much deeper form of the real. It has us circling back to where we came from, to the place where we started out.

Only by turning *twice* can we begin to engage with the world as the gods do—facing toward suffering rather than away from it. This is how we become like them—the Boddhisatvas, the gods, those who have eternal life.

In other words, only when we no longer think of heaven as a goal do we begin to appreciate what walking *with* (rather than *toward*) the enlightened ones might be. Like them, we have turned ourselves around and are now ready to deal with the troubles that lie before us, rather than behind us. Having experienced this necessary rebellion, this second turning, our goal becomes not escaping from sin but engaging with a sinful world.

This full engagement is the end (and purpose) of the world. It is nothingness, purpose without purpose, a shared fullness that lies well beyond sense and reason.

The covenant path takes us back to the burning house. It requires condescension, kenosis, a loss of self. As the poet Matsuo Bashō (1644–94) put it, "Knowing the high, we return to the low." By embracing nothingness, we become mediators for others. Even Jesus in his moment of turning, when he looked to heaven and asked if his sacrifice had to be, needed to decide. Only after this moment of questioning did he let himself be nailed to a cross. He died, turned away from heaven and toward his mother, toward his disciples, toward the women he loved, toward the soldiers, toward the crowd that came to watch him die.

Again, we, too, must turn *twice*—once to God and once away from God, once toward the truth and then, after this, toward true life. Only by pushing through sorrow, only by asking *all* the questions that the gods have placed in our hearts—the usual ones and the unusual ones—only by feeling the pain and godly sorrow of justice, do we begin to learn the meaning of the Atonement.

And when we do, we take our own place between the demands of justice, on the one side, and those who are to be punished because of their failings, on the other. We take the middle position. Like Jesus, we become mediators. As such, we return to the burning house for the most obvious of reasons. What good is salvation if those we love are not saved?

How could we let Uncle Bob just sit there in the burning house, watching television and eating chips? Just when we gain the ability to leave this world of suffering, we decide to stay.

> five tubs of wheat—
> in the dawning light
> the robins sing

We are taught that there is a season for everything. Similarly, to every discourse there is a method—a set of relevant questions that yield certain kinds of answers and patterns of behavior. What is life? What is gravity? What is consciousness? How does a radio work?

You can remove a spark plug with a pipe wrench, but that is not what it was designed to do. An adjustable wrench is widely useful, but a real mechanic knows the limitations of such a flexible tool.

"Does God exist?" This not a religious question. It never was. It never will be.

"How do the gods feel about me?" This is a religious question and a tool of faith. "How do I feel about them?" This also is. "What does it mean to believe in things?" This is not. "Do I understand faith and what it means to have faith?" This is.

I am walking out of the library. I have just heard the announcement that the restriction that kept Blacks from holding the priesthood has been lifted. I remember my time with Spencer W. Kimball in Sapporo. I recall the humble pureness of his heart and realize it took his kind of clarity to lead the effort that led to this revelation.

A great burden is lifted from me. In this and other matters, I come to understand that many of the things I struggle with as a Latter-day Saint are caused not by the gospel but by the modern cultural context in which "the stone cut from the mountain" has to unfold. The cultural environment that has long vitiated the simple teachings of Jesus is still dust on the feet of anyone who would walk the path of righteousness.

I am always surprised when spiritually minded people aspire to be modern. Don't they understand that modernity is secular? Modern culture is not a friend to faith. It hasn't been. It isn't now. It will never be.

I take up dancing again. Karen Johnson, an anthropology PhD candidate, finds out about my premissionary past. One late afternoon, the two of us meet in an unoccupied classroom. In the shadows of the sandstone columns, she sets up her boom box. We push back the chairs. She teaches me a few moves.

After two or three sessions, we're ready. We make our debut at a place in San Francisco called Dance Your Ass Off. I love the lighted floor, the rising fog, the syncopated bass, the sappy violins, the slim waiters balancing round trays of drinks with one hand. *Saturday Night Fever* is all the rage. The disco craze is on!

I team up with Linda Uyechi, another member of the Stanford Ward, also an undergraduate. We win second place at the People's Disco Contest. We can't beat the tight, rhythmic precision of the Latin dancers, but we think we have more fun than they do (or so we tell ourselves).

> gimme that night
> fever night fevaaah—
> El Camino Real

Back to Japan, Taipei, Enlightenment

DURING MY FINAL MONTHS AT STANFORD, I APPLY FOR AND receive a Monbushō Scholarship. For the next three and a half years, I will study in Japan with Noguchi Takehiko, famed scholar of Japanese literature.

All my expenses are paid by the Japanese Ministry of Education. I have all the resources I need to continue my exploration of the world. On this second trip to Japan, I hope to learn what I should have learned on my first trip but didn't. This time, Zion or bust.

I need to know one thing and one thing only. How do people live? I need to emerge from my shell and learn how my brothers and sisters experience the world. What are their lives like? What do they love and hate? I will not shy away from understanding anyone. Not this time. Not anymore. This is what Jesus wants me to do. This is what Zen will lead me to. This is how Zion will happen.

*

I find myself in a dormitory for foreign students in Kita Senri, a commuter town located between Osaka and Kyoto. All of us are in our twenties. We are from every part of the world—South America, the Middle East, Southeast Asia, Europe, Australia. We are a radically diverse community of learners, all future leaders in our various fields. Our energy is limitless, as is our desire to have a good time.

Our parties are wild. The one kind of music that everyone enjoys is not the Bee Gees but South American carnival music. After our dances, the paper cups and plates on the floor are a foot deep.

I travel to Kobe to meet my professors for the first time. We sit at a square table in a small room filled with shelves of books. Professors Noguchi and Sōma smoke cigarettes and drink tea. I sit quietly with my hands on my lap. No one says much of anything.

Feeling very uncomfortable, I tell myself, "Just follow their lead."

A few weeks later, as soon as classes start, I move out of the dorm to live in Kobe, closer to my university. I say goodbye to my newly found friends. The person I will miss most is Cecile Leon, daughter of a Parisian painter. She studies Chinese poetry and is as urbane as I am rustic. I find myself drawn to her sophistication like a moth to a candle.

*

I end up in a small, cockroach-infested studio apartment about a ten-minute walk from campus. The six-unit building is built against a cliff. It gets very little sunlight, even at midday. Although it has a poetic name, Bizan-sō, the place is definitely low-rent.

My neighbors include a young couple, a cook at a Kobe beef shop, and an older single woman who cooks for me once a week in exchange for English lessons. There is also an expat English teacher from Michigan, and an Okinawan woman from Honolulu who also teaches English.

At night, after I lay out my futon in the middle of the room, I turn off the lights and watch the cockroaches cautiously emerge from the corners.

> eleven pm—
> a slumber party for six
> or seven or eight

Did anyone bring popcorn?

*

I hear my neighbors through the walls, which are very thin. At night, they embrace passionately. During the day, the wife plays Elvis Presley. Their five-year-old daughter has a pet turtle, which she keeps in a plastic container slightly larger than the turtle itself. Every time I leave my apartment, I walk past the captive animal and my spirit groans.

> the crows all say
> "hey, mind your own business"—
> autumn willows sway

One day, I can't stand it any longer. I tip over the container and spill out the water. I try to make things look as if the turtle escaped on its own power.

I release the animal in a garden pond across the street. The neighbor girl cries and cries when she discovers her pet missing. I'm sure she suspects me of wrongdoing, but no one asks me about it.

Mori Haruhide, professor of English at Kobe University, invites me to live in his mother-in-law's newly built home in Mikage. At some point in the future, the house will become her place of retirement. But for a few more years, she'll continue living in downtown Kobe.

Mori needs someone to live in the house and to water the garden. He likes me because I'm a foreigner with zero furniture of my own. He's also hoping I'll translate his book on D. H. Lawrence from Japanese into English.

At his bidding, I take a look at the place. It's a strangely romantic cottage, straight out of a Grimms' fairy tale. Inside, it has lots of shiny woodwork, including a large built-in bookshelf. So far, the only volumes on the shelves are the complete works of Natsume Sōseki.

The garden outside is carefully landscaped and filled with exotic plants. It's on a hill overlooking the ocean.

I move out of Bizan-sō and into this luxurious abode. The tatami is still green, and the resin in the wood is fragrant. My desk overlooks Osaka Bay. When I look up from my books, I can see many ships. Port Island and the Kansai International Airport are rising out of the sea in the distance, one boatload of fill at a time. Debussy's "La soirée dans Grenade" plays on my Walkman.

The setting is stunning.

Conditions could not be better. And yet, my life in Mikage is far from cheerful. Every day, I get up. I read and read and read. I jump on my motorcycle and go to classes. I drive back up the hill. I climb the stairway to the second floor, where I lie down in bed and try to fall asleep.

I have no one to talk to. My only companion is a cricket who lives in the ivy just outside my window. Every night I listen to him sing, and I wonder, "How long will you be with me?"

Autumn deepens. The weather grows steadily colder. One night the singing stops.

> farewell my friend—
> outside my autumn window
> a chilling silence

I am far from home and feeling completely alone. I'm learning an important lesson the hard way. As the temple ceremony teaches all who go there to learn about the purpose of human existence, "It is not good for man to be alone."

When I was a missionary, I used to suffer from yellow-window syndrome. I would pass by someone's house at night and see warm light coming from inside. I would think of the happy lives of the people living there, and I would miss my family.

That feeling of separation returns. Once again, I am lonely. But now there's a big difference. I'm old enough to realize that the family I most want to be with is the one I will have to create myself. My instinct to retreat from others will certainly not get me there!

*

I am desperate for family life. I often visit the home of Hide and Vickie Aida. They are a young, newly married couple with a baby boy named Justin. We attend the same tiny English-speaking Kobe Branch on Sundays. Being with them makes me happy, even though I know my visits are an imposition.

I wish I were happily married like they are.

I begin to date. But I am not really present for the people I try to love. Even as I complain about my solitude, I'm incapable of caring about others wholeheartedly. Annie would say that I'm still thinking too much. I am in love with the idea of love. My romanticism is a freeway to no particular person or destination.

My relationship with Noguchi-sensei also causes me concern. He and I might be alike in our level of dedication to literature, but in other ways, we couldn't be more different. For one thing, he's a famous alcoholic, and I don't drink at all.

I'm still a Latter-day Saint, attending meetings every Sunday.

Professor Mori is not happy with me. Because I'm making little progress translating his book, they finally ask me to move out. I find a new place. It's a grimy, one-room apartment near the Hankyū Rokko Station, just down the hill from the university. This place is a much better fit. I'm in the thick of urban life. The flower vendor comes by every afternoon with his cart of freshly cut peonies. Every night at about 1:00 a.m., the "cat lady" meets with her followers outside my apartment window.

One night, I finally get tired of this woman who loves cats. I open the window. The moonlight pours into my apartment, very blue. She is standing there in the street, not more than a few yards away. Three or four cats, all of them sitting in a semicircle, are looking at her.

She looks back over her shoulder at me.

"What time do you think it is, anyway?" I ask.

"*Ara*," she replies. "My goodness."

She faces her cats. "Apologize to this nice young man. We've been keeping him up."

Speaking on her behalf, the cats say they are very sorry for the noise.

Noguchi-sensei visits one morning. He's been drinking all night. I'm up early making breakfast.

He sits at my desk and studies my movements.

I fry an egg. I pour a glass of tangerine juice. I toast a thick slice of white bread and put some strawberry jam on it.

"Are you sure you don't want something?" I offer to make him breakfast too.

He retorts, "You're the healthiest guy I've ever seen." ("*Konna kenzen na yatsu wo mita koto ga nai.*") It's not a compliment, actually.

I admit it. I am pretty healthy.

I eat Bulgarian yogurt. I purchase dark German bread when I can get it. My noon meal is usually the B Lunch at the Chinese place near Rokko Station—plenty of vegetables. But the nuance of his word *kenzen* is quite a bit wider than just "healthy."

What he really objects to is my refusal to drink with him. I'm sure he thinks I'm being unfriendly. And he's right. From his point of view, I certainly am. There's no other way to put it.

I find myself wondering. "Which is worse? Offending someone who is trying to be my friend? Or not following God's every commandment with perfect exactness?" After all, it's not like the gods are on one side, and people are on the other. But then there's the example of Joseph Smith and Martin Harris, how they lost the manuscript pages for the first section of the Book of Mormon because Joseph feared man more than God.

I'm torn.

*

It's Thursday afternoon. Our graduate seminar is over. Noguchi-sensei takes us all drinking, as is his custom.

We walk down the hill to a *konomi-yaki* (savory pancake) shop a few blocks away. Everyone eats a little and has a few beers. We pile into taxis and head for Sannomiya. We get out of the cars and make our way through a maze of narrow alleys and small shops.

Sensei prefers one-room bars run by elderly women, probably because he can tell them to put his drinking bill on a tab. (When he wins the Suntory Prize for one of his books, he uses the prize money to pay off all his drinking debts. So he actually is sincere about paying what he owes.)

His preferred drink is bourbon. Every Thursday night, he consumes a fifth of it.

I drink orange soda.

I realize that I like Noguchi-sensei best when he's a little drunk. The edge comes off, and he's easier to talk to. By the end of the evening, though, after he's downed that fifth of Jim Beam, he's like a jellyfish. Our evenings often end with two or three of us lugging him to a taxi and throwing him in.

As burdensome as that might sound, I attend these drinking sessions faithfully. As I've said, I'm lonely. Not only that, but in

Japan this is usually how friendship begins, when everyone has had something to drink.

*

About a year later, I've successfully gotten into the master's program in Japanese literature and am attending a department party at the university. In my hand, I hold a plastic cup partially filled with Kirin beer. I've learned that it's easier to go through the motions than try to explain why you don't drink. People don't bother you as long as your cup has something in it.

On this particular day, though, the solitude of my life as a foreign student finally gets to me. I take a sip. Memories of high school come flooding back. Good thing Kirk Andersen's dad, who was the Gunnison city cop back when we were sixteen, didn't throw us all in jail that night he pulled us over. Our lives would have been very different had justice been done. (And it certainly would have been done had we been young black men.)

Professor Noguchi comes by and looks at my cup. A smile comes across his lips. Only he would notice that the level has changed ever so slightly. "Charlie," he says. "You're a soft Mormon."

At last, I have fallen. I don't have much to say in my defense. I feel ashamed.

He walks away. Halfway across the room, he stops, turns, and comes back to where I am still standing. He adds, "A soft Mormon. Isn't that a little like being a soft Stalinist?"

He turns again and walks away, proud of his joke.

> "Leave them alone!"—
> the pioneers in St. George
> loved their grape juice

Years later, Noguchi-sensei eventually has to quit drinking and smoking for health reasons. Surprisingly, the drastic change does not seem to make a dent in his productivity, which remains nothing short of phenomenal. It doesn't alter his personality either.

He's just a remarkable person. A genius. There's no other way to put it.

After two and a half more years in Kobe, I finish my master's degree. My parents come to Japan for the ceremony. After having dinner with Sensei and his wife, Yoshiko, at their home in Ashiya, my father comments, "Intellectual sharpness isn't the only thing to strive for."

My parents meet my other friends. My father tells me I should marry Sandra Murayama, a Japanese girl from Brazil. She's pretty, polite, and has incredible language skills. The thought has crossed my mind, actually. But, like I say, I'm still too in love with love to devote myself to any one person in particular.

*

I see my father and mother off at the airport.

The man at the Japanese Airline counter gives them two carry-on baggage tags and says, "*Kore wo tsukete kudasai.*" ("Put these on, please.")

I go off to buy some snacks. When I come back, there they are. My mother and father are standing side by side, each with a tag on the right wrist.

I laugh. I cry.

> on their wedding night—
> did my parents exchange
> serial numbers?

I'm going to miss Japan. I visit Kyoto one last time. At the Ryōanji, a Zen temple on the west side of town, I pay my 300 yen. I get a pamphlet. I take off my shoes and sit down on the wooden veranda that overlooks the famous rock garden.

I read, "Look at the garden. What do you see? Rocks and gravel? Or do you see the tips of mountains jutting above the clouds? Or islands in the swirling sea?"

"Okay, I get it." The garden as cosmos.

Later that same day, I travel to the Nanzenji on the other side of the city. The garden is magnificent, punctuated with rocks, trees, and areas of raked gravel. I point to the careful, perfectly parallel lines and ask the guide, "What do these lines in the gravel mean?" Secretly, I'm hoping to display some of my newly acquired knowledge.

She doesn't answer right away.

I think to myself, "Currents in a stream? A glacier carving its way down a Norwegian fjord?"

She finally responds. "It means, sir, stay off the gravel."

✳

A month before my departure date, the doorbell rings. I am now living in an apartment in Shinohara honmachi, on the Sannomiya side of Rokko Station. The Tsukudas have been my friends pretty much the entire time I've been in Kobe. They tear down their house and put up a multistory apartment building. They let me stay in one unit on the first floor, where they keep their stash of Amway products. Mrs. Tsukuda, who gets in at the top of the pyramid scheme, eventually makes a fortune. Mr. Tsukuda plays jazz piano at a local nightclub.

I go to the door. It's my neighbor, a woman I occasionally bump into on the street. My guess is that she's in her early fifties, but she's very youthful. I always think she dresses much too young for her age.

She introduces herself, and hands me an envelope. "I want you to date my daughter."

"You what?"

The woman is Korean. Her Japanese is not that great. She keeps saying, "With a clean heart. With a clean heart." (*"Kirei na kimochi de."*)

I see that the envelope is filled with the equivalent of hundred-dollar bills.

She explains. Her husband is old-fashioned. At some point, he'll tell their daughter to marry some man he has chosen for her, and she will do as he says. She has no choice.

"So what does this have to do with me?"

"I want you to show my daughter a good time. You know, what it feels like to be on a date."

"Why me?"

"I've been watching you," she says. "I know I can trust you."

I don't know what to say. "Look, I'm happy to meet your daughter, if that's what you want. You don't have to pay me for it. Really."

I try to hand the envelope back to her.

"With a clean heart," she says again, pushing the envelope back my way. "We own a pachinko parlor in Osaka. My husband gives me this money every month, and I don't know what to do with it all. I want you to have it, as a token of my appreciation."

She says goodbye and walks away.

I go back inside, envelope in hand.

I sit down at my desk and count out the bills. It's just enough to ship all my books back to the States. For the past three years, I've been paying tithing on my scholarship money, and now the promised blessing comes (see Malachi 3:8–10).

> a mother's deep love—
> pachinko's richest blessings
> for the boy next door

We go on a date, but it isn't much fun. The daughter confronts me, and I tell her the truth.

I take the long way home. I travel to Taipei to study Mandarin at Tai-Da for a few months before returning to America.

I like this city. The mounds of fresh fruit piled on the Taipei streets are impressive. So is the Babaobing, the "Eight Jeweled Ice"—shaved ice with eight different toppings. It's the most perfectly refreshing thing to eat on a hot tropical day.

I live with Doctor Ch'en and his family, right across the street from the Dragon Mountain Temple in Ximending. It's a colorful, old part of town. Snake Alley and the brothels are just two or three blocks away.

I meet Robert Christensen, a Princeton ABD (having completed all but his dissertation). We ride around town on his Vespa scooter and eat pork chops.

*

With Robert, I attend a small Latter-day Saint ward for foreigners. We're a motley collection of entrepreneurs, students, and members of the mission president's family. I never learn the president's name, and he doesn't learn mine. He's very unfriendly. Back in the States, he owns a chain of pie stores. But now, for three years, he's directing the missionary effort in the northern part of Taiwan. He does not approve of young, unattached males—and that is what I am.

One of the few other older men in the ward, Brother Ebers, wears perfectly ironed white shirts, set off with US Senate cufflinks and a matching tie tack. His hair is a little on the oily side, long and combed back. Sister Ebers is friendly and nice-looking. She says hello to everyone.

There are a few more married couples, all quite a bit younger. One lives in a marble mansion not too far from the meetinghouse. The husband tells me that he grew up poor. "My dad used to make garbage soup once a week. Anything he found in the refrigerator, he'd throw into a pot."

Right after his mission, he got the brilliant idea to make the head of tennis racquets a little bigger so it would be easier to hit the ball. Because he successfully filed a patent on the idea, he gets a cut whenever anyone makes a tennis racquet with a bigger hitting area (which is anytime anybody makes a tennis racquet). Bingo. Instant fortune!

Another young couple is much less affluent. The husband is a former Green Beret who did three tours in Vietnam. He's still in fighting shape and is a recent convert. He tells me, "You missionaries are the real warriors of the world. You're the ones who do the real fighting." His wife is Chinese. She's gracious and warm. Like her husband, she's also very gentle and kind.

There is also a group of college students who are participating in a BYU summer program. Most of them are coeds, but one is a confident young man from southern California. He has short, dark brown hair, and an inexhaustible wardrobe of form-fitting clothes. Even on the sabbath, he wears colorful shirts that are open at the collar.

One Sunday morning, the bishop chooses to put this young man on the spot. He calls him to the podium and asks him to bear his testimony about the blessings of marriage. "Tell us about your ideal woman, Brother Tadesko."

He reluctantly accepts the challenge. Men his age (and mine) are supposed to be married. So there's nothing subtle about what the bishop's up to. He's asking him to get with the program.

The young man stands at the podium. The room is small. No microphone required.

He flashes a smile. Very nice teeth.

"Well, since you asked, Bishop. How about an older woman? Maybe a rich widow. That would be nice."

He gets a few laughs and sits down.

The bishop is undaunted. He calls next on Sister Ebers, the one married to the coal trader with apparent Senate connections. Same topic.

"Well, I just love Brother Ebers," she begins, then goes on to enumerate her husband's many virtues. She tells us about how marriage takes work, how you change over time. "You learn and grow. I no longer say to Brother Ebers, 'Dear, you should have bought the Chicago Bears.'"

She ends with her testimony. Jesus is the Christ. This is his true church.

She sits down.

The bishop only has to nod and smile at the next speaker.

Brother Ebers slowly rises. He comes to the front of the room, bringing a full load of dignity with him. He grips the edges of the podium and leans forward a little. He takes us into his gaze. The sleeves of his jacket pull back, exposing his gleaming US Senate cufflinks. He acknowledges his wife and begins.

"Good morning, brothers and sisters. It is good to be here."

We learn that they're originally from Chicago. After successes in this and that business venture, they now live in the Peace Hotel, which is the largest, nicest accommodation in the city. He makes a "decent living" by buying and shipping boatloads of coal to Taiwan.

He thanks God for his beautiful wife. "Our children understand that Saturday morning is the time when Sister Ebers and I cuddle." He smiles. "You young people, marriage is a blessing. Don't be afraid of it."

He goes on. "I, too, know that the gospel is true. That Jesus is the Christ. And I can testify to you that Sister Ebers," his tempo slows for emphasis, "makes *sweet, sweet* love."

Just then, someone outside the building lights a long string of firecrackers. *Pop, pop, pop, pop, pop.* The Taiwanese don't kid around when it comes to celebratory explosives. The string of rapid blasts lasts for a full minute. Smoke rises from the street below and enters through the open windows. The room breaks into pandemonium.

Scandalized by Brother Ebers's candor, the BYU students nervously laugh. Some of the women hug each other. The mission president scowls at this outbreak of disorder and looks nervously left and right. He starts nervously reaching out, as if he's forgotten where he put something. His scriptures? Or maybe his pistol?

Unphased by the firecrackers, Brother Ebers calmly stands his ground before us. He's been in Taiwan long enough to know what's coming. Finally, the last of the firecrackers sputter and pop, ending in one extra loud *BOOM!*

Ebers looks at us through the bluish smoke. He smiles and says, "Amen," then takes his seat.

> the big bang theory—
> inside the smoke-filled chapel
> a satisfied smile

One week before returning to America, I am riding in a broken-down aluminum bus as it rattles across the city. The Taipei traffic is terrible. Men pass by on their motorbikes. Their wives and children are on board with them. Nobody is wearing a helmet.

My Sony Walkman is playing Billy Joel's greatest hits. "Bottle of red, bottle of white, it all depends on your appetite . . ." Suddenly, I am filled with a feeling of great happiness. It's like I've stepped into a shower of perfect water. Euphoria washes away all my doubts. My sins, my insecurities all vanish. I hear a familiar voice whispering to me once again. "I gave you this time to learn about the world. So what has it taught you?"

In a word, what my three and a half years of living dangerously have taught me is the need for forgiveness and compassion. I think I've learned a lot about how not to be judgmental, about why I shouldn't hold the world at arm's length. In my desire to understand the world, I admit that I've strayed a bit from the beaten path. But I also know that I've done so with a purpose that never left my mind the entire time.

"Yes," I think to myself, "I'm finally beginning to understand how it all works. I am now starting to figure out how to be *in* the world without being *of* it."

Jesus knew the sorrows of sin, and he came to this understanding without sinning. But for the rest of us, there is no other way.

I look around at the people in the bus. I realize that this warm sensation that fills my heart is God's love, pure and simple. I begin to weep. The feeling is overwhelming. I feel real joy. This must be how Lehi felt when he partook of the fruit from the tree of life. Through my tears, I remember my first experience with sugar cookies. I recall the sweet generosity of the sisters in Sigurd and am filled with a desire to hug everyone on the bus.

A bottomless, unconditional feeling of gratitude lifts me from my seat. I feel a depth of compassion that goes far beyond anything I have ever felt before. This is it. This is what I have been wanting to know, all these years.

Is this how God feels about his children? Is this the design of Zion Earth and Zen Sky, the lines put down in the sand, the creative answer to all things decaying?

> turn down the volume—
> that woman sitting there is
> your sister in heaven
>
> riding God's bus—
> my tears are brighter than
> steel and aluminum
>
> swirling yin and yang—
> traffic oozes around a
> Taipei rotary

CHAPTER 11

Marriage, Mie

I RETURN TO AMERICA. I AM READY TO MOVE AHEAD. AT Noguchi-sensei's recommendation, my next mentor will be Howard Hibbett, Victor S. Thomas Professor of Japanese Literature at Harvard University. He is the translator of Tanizaki Jun'ichirō's *The Key*. Like Noguchi, Hibbett is brilliant but also hard to know. Our friendship grows slowly, but it keeps developing steadily for many years to come.

Cambridge also takes some getting used to. I'm not accustomed to hearing so many sirens, nor do I understand the driving patterns. For one thing, the streets are narrow and sometimes change their names as you go from one town to the next. There are also many one-way streets, which means that I have to ask myself which store in Harvard Square I want to go to before planning a trip there. And the way there is never the way back.

One morning I'm commuting to Harvard. I'm riding my bicycle down Cambridge Street when a man, also on a bike, snarls at me as he passes by. For what? Am I in his way?

In Cambridge, Massachusetts, age 25.

I pedal faster and pull up beside him, "What's your problem?" I ask.

Maybe it's because I'm a graduate student, filling my head with critiques of hegemony and structural racism, that makes me take offense. Or is it just the narrowness of the street and the dangerous mix of vehicles? Whatever it is, the man's rudeness bothers me.

I peddle beside him, "What's your problem?"

He snarls at me again, then looks away. This makes me even angrier.

Having just lived in Japan for three and a half years, I see America differently now. I know that there are places in the world where the people are more like me than like this white guy.

I make a plan. I'll ride up beside him, knock him off his bike, and beat him up, right there on Cambridge Street. I'll do it for everyone to see. I'll do it for my grandparents, for my parents, for all the Japanese Americans who were unjustly imprisoned during the War. I'll take him down and teach him a lesson he'll never forget.

"That man will never disrespect people like me again," I think.

I pull up close. Just as I am about to launch my attack, a city bus roars up from behind and swerves over to the curb. We both have to steer out of the way to avoid getting hit.

We recover. We start pedaling again. I have him in my sights. I close in on him again. For the second time, I'm about to push the guy off his bicycle, when the same bus comes roaring up. Once more, it suddenly swerves over to the curb to pick up more passengers. Again, we steer to get out of the way. The bus barely misses us.

The white guy regains his balance. So do I. He continues down the road. I pursue.

I catch up to him a third time. I'm just about to kick his bicycle over with my right foot, when the same bus comes from behind a third time. Again it swerves over to the curb, nearly hitting us. It seems that the speed of our travel perfectly matches the frequency of the bus picking up and discharging passengers.

This pattern promises to continue all the way to Harvard, but this time the man says, "That son of a bitch is going to kill us both."

And then I laugh.

And he laughs too.

The second we laugh together, my hatred suddenly leaves me. "What are you doing, Charles?"

The Holy Ghost tells me to let him go. I obey.

He goes his way. I go mine.

How foolish and wrong of me to judge that man! Even if he disrespects me, I know I must pray for his happiness and for the happiness of his family. I must love him. One more lesson learned.

I meet a woman whose hair is so brilliant that it hurts my eyes. She bakes me a loaf of challah. After six months of dating, we get married. On our honeymoon, I misplace my car keys many times. Two years later, we have our first child, a little girl.

I am driving home after a long night in the Brigham and Women's Hospital. Like many first-time parents, we go to the hospital way too early. I don't like to waste time, so I donate blood while I'm waiting. By midnight, when contractions begin in earnest, I am totally exhausted.

I remember the nurses preparing the stainless steel pan that catches the baby as it comes out. It's a slightly larger version of those scoops they weigh nails in at a hardware store. Seeing it, I realize, "Wow, we are really going to have a baby."

*

I'm on my way home. It's going to feel so good to eat something warm, to take a shower, and to get some sleep.

I turn the corner near our apartment on Cambridge Street, near the Youville Hospital. I see a homeless man. He's dressed in a bulky, dark coat, lying on a bus stop bench.

A thought comes to me. "Everyone is somebody's baby." Sounds like the title of a song. But the point is, that man was once a baby too. Everyone in this world is someone's baby.

I wonder. Do other parents feel about their children like I feel about my daughter? My love for her is immediate and enormous. It changes me forever.

We name our baby Mie. Depending on the characters used, the name could mean "fruitful branch" or "beautiful blessing," 実枝 or 美恵. Either is fine, though I prefer the former. I'm partial to plants and to anything fractal, including the universe. We decide to let Mie decide for herself someday.

> it's a baby girl—
> blossoms in springtime
> fruit in the fall

Marriage changes many things, but not all things. At my request, we still spend summers on the farm. I feel obligated to help my parents, who are slowing with age. I also feel bad about not taking over the family business. And then there is the matter of needing money to get through grad school. Even buying groceries is a week-to-week challenge.

The silence of rural Utah is also the same as ever. The first time we visit Gunnison together, my wife steps out of the car and immediately begins to cry.

"What's wrong?" I ask. "Are you okay?"

"It's so quiet here." As the daughter of a famous composer and an accomplished painter, she feels the loneliness too. That's one of the many reasons I asked her to marry me.

One afternoon on the farm, while pressure washing a grain combine, I carelessly get my hand caught in a spinning gear. The pointing finger on my left hand is ripped open halfway down to my palm. The bone sticks out of the bloody mess, exposed and snapped off.

> how ghostly white—
> my shattered fingerbone points
> to the cloudless sky

My father rushes me to the hospital. Dwight, now a country doctor, happens to be on call. He thoroughly scrubs the crushed pieces of my finger, then attempts a reconstruction. I almost pass out because of the pain.

"If I send you north to the specialists, they'll just chop it off here," he explains, pointing to the first joint.

Dwight is good with a needle and thread. One stitch at a time, my finger starts to look like a finger again. Over the next two weeks, most of the tissue gets enough circulation to live. But the tip becomes infected. It dies and eventually hardens and falls off.

I begin to envy people who are still fully base ten.

> the newscaster's hands—
> my injured finger throbs
> whenever I yawn

My wife is concerned that I work too hard. She buys me a fly rod from Stoddard's cutlery shop in downtown Boston. Maybe I'll learn how to relax.

Her generous plan backfires, though, because now I have two obsessions rather than one.

I love everything about Japanese literature *and* fly fishing. I'm mesmerized by the way a fly line curls in the air and by the sight of a trout taking a dry fly from the surface of a stream. Such moments remind me that, despite my love of language and literature, I am still an animal. I am still a thing.

During our summer visits to Utah, I visit a few small creeks where nobody goes. One summer evening in July, I'm walking back to where I parked my truck. My waders quickly dry in the cooling Utah air.

I set my rod down and pause on a rocky outflow of igneous rock. I sit down on a boulder and take a rest. As the sun sets, I feel a perfect stillness. I sense the strength of the earth at that magical spot.

> in Piute County—
> the dark rocks on the hillside
> are filled with sunlight

This is a holy place. Henry's ancestors probably stood here, looking down at the river below, understanding their dependence on the earth for its bounty of deer and trout, pine nuts and other seeds.

Our planet has many such spots. In Japan, they are often marked with *shimenawa*, straw ropes with tassels and lightning-shaped paper markers. You find them tied around trees and rocks that have an especially strong spirit. Having survived the positivism of the modern era, the animistic foundations of Japanese culture still make themselves known today by way of these primitive markers.

Such powerful places exist in America as well. But they are not as formalized, or as commonly revered. As a general rule, few things here are as formalized as they are in Japan.

CHAPTER 12

Home Teaching, Bashō

Slowly, I learn to trust God enough to do what he asks of me—to accept callings to serve, to align myself with his will, to repent of the things that keep me walled off from others. I decide to do my home teaching with sincere intent. As I "feed his sheep," the miracles begin to flow.

Back in the States, one of the people I'm assigned to minister to is Ruby Von Dwornik. She lives on the fourth floor of a walk-up near Harvard Law School. Mie and I are walking her dog while she takes care of her husband Daniel, who is seriously ill.

I'm still in graduate school. Mie is five or six.

As we come up the stairs, Ruby meets us in the stairwell. "Daniel just passed," she says.

I look at Ruby, not knowing what to say. Then I understand. She wants to give me a chance to decide. Do I want to let my daughter see a dead person or not?

I look at Mie and think for a minute. "If I don't take her into that apartment, she'll always wonder, 'What was it that Daddy didn't want me to see?'"

Ruby, Mie, Ruby's dog, and I climb the rest of the stairs and walk into the apartment. Daniel is there, lying in his bed. His face is pale. He is no longer breathing. Outside the windows, the leaves of the walnut tree are just coming on.

Ruby is beside herself with grief. Over the past few months, she has witnessed the sudden decline and death of her husband. Because I am her home teacher, assigned to visit her once a month, I have experienced this sadness with her.

> promising spring—
> the sugar maple and
> forsythia bloom

On the face of it, nothing is so false as an assigned friendship. Yet being a home teacher to Ruby is raking gravel in its very essence. Our designated connection is a godly way to help people like me learn how to overcome a tendency to avoid others. I know that, left alone, my life would become increasingly limited. Not knowing God's gentle commands, I would seek association with those who share my values and experiences. I would avoid all others. As a result, my life would steadily become narrower and more impoverished. I would slowly lose real human interaction and understanding.

For most people, this poverty of experience is what adulthood is all about. At some point, usually in our twenties, we decide that we are liberal or conservative, religious or secular, fated to be rich or bound to be poor. Being one thing, we stop being another. Few things are as depressing as the way life narrows as we age.

I wish it were not so, but this is how it usually goes. Ruby and I would not have become friends had I not been given a commandment from God to befriend her. One thing this tells me is that

Homo sapiens are not sapient enough to live without commandments to follow. God loves us, so he hands us a rake and asks us to get this and that job done.

Ruby goes away to California for a few weeks and comes back. In her moment of greatest need, I take her to see Bishop Hangen. We give her a blessing of comfort, and the Spirit sips her agony away.

> after the blessing—
> we no longer hear the sounds
> of cars on Mass Ave

I am called to be a Sunday School teacher in the Cambridge First Ward. The first day on the job, I try to make an important point: there are different ways to read the scriptures. The Old Testament in particular can sometimes be a very literary text.

I write a question on the board, "How big is God?"

I point to a passage from the Pearl of Great Price. "Wherefore Enoch saw that Noah built an ark; and that the Lord smiled upon it, and held it in his own hand; but upon the residue of the wicked the floods came and swallowed them up" (Moses 7:43).

"Now, if we assume that people have been made in God's image, as the Bible says, and if we know the usual proportions of the hand to the rest of the human body, then we can calculate the height of God. This is because in yet another passage in the Bible we are told the precise measurements of the ark: 300 cubits long. So if a cubit is about twenty inches, and God's hand is approximately the same length as the ship—300 x 20 inches long, or about 500 feet—then, given the proportions of the hand to the rest of the body, say about 1 to 10, his total height would be something like 5,000 feet."

I do the calculations on the board. "So there you have it. That's how big God is. Five thousand feet tall. He must have been a great basketball player in his day."

The classroom grows quiet. No one really knows what to say.

Finally, Bill Cortelyou, a Boston taxi driver who spreads the gospel by throwing copies of the Book of Mormon at people standing on the curb as he drives by, raises his hand and says, "I don't like it."

"Excuse me?"

"I don't like your answer."

This is, of course, the response I anticipated. "Why not?"

"You do things like that, Brother Inouye, and—I dunno, everything gets flimsy."

"Exactly. So my point is that we *shouldn't* take everything so literally. Some things, yes. Other things, no. This phrase, God holding the ark in his hand, is a metaphor for his caring for Noah and his family, and by extension, for you and me. It's not a tip-off about how tall he is. Right?"

Bill still doesn't quite get my point. After class, I try to explain it to him. I also apologize for the confusion. I feel bad about this moment of difficulty. For him, my offering was too clever to be helpful.

*

The Sunday School president gets word of my unusual lesson. He begins monitoring my classes. He stands in the back of the classroom with his hands on his hips, never saying a word. After a few visits, he complains to Bishop Satō and asks that I be released.

The bishop resists. But the Sunday School president insists.

His importunity forces a special fast and prayer. Bishop Satō and his counselors kneel in his office and pray for guidance. Should they release Charles from his calling as a Sunday School teacher or not?

Of course, all of this happens without my knowing it. Only months later does one of my friends, my mole in the bishopric, tell me what happened. "Yeah. We all felt the Spirit, and I guess we decided not to dump your sorry soul. I don't know why, Brother Inouye. But God loves you for some reason."

My response to this news is complicated. I feel every possible emotion, from gratitude to irritation. I also feel chastened. I realize the need to "preach nothing save it were repentance and faith on the Lord, who had redeemed his people" (Mosiah 18:20). By and by, I also come to understand that for teaching to be effective, the Spirit has to be present. That's the most important thing. Good teaching happens when *all* are edified (Doctrine and Covenants 50:22–23). I eventually figure out that this applies to the university classroom as much as it does to the Sunday School classroom.

Authenticity, yes. Manipulation, no.

We move from Cambridge to 378 Massachusetts Avenue in Lexington. Our home ward changes, as does my home teaching route. I am assigned to be the Duke family's home teacher.

The Dukes live in Arlington, not far from the high school. They are active members. Kerry is a member of the bishopric, and Amy used to be a Relief Society president.

My visits to them are rather routine until, one afternoon after church, Kerry has a heart attack and dies. He leaves behind his wife and four young children—Taylor, Wesley, Erin, and Kyle.

We are all devastated by Kerry's sudden passing. At the wake, Amy stands next to the casket, dressed in black, her corsage crushed by the hundreds of people who hug her as they file by to pay their respects. I feel for her, and for the children. They are suddenly without a father.

Two weeks after the funeral, I am working in my study. It is about seven in the morning. The sunlight filters through the rectangular pieces of Japanese paper that we have taped on the windowpanes to keep the glare out. I feel a presence in the room. I look to the left, and there is Kerry standing next to me.

*

I have always believed in life after death. But I have never met a dead person before.

Kerry is not glowing brightly, as angels are sometimes portrayed in paintings and other media. There is a slight translucence to his body, but he definitely belongs to the material world. He sends me a message—a flow of intelligence from his mind to mine. He wants me to take care of his family now that he is no longer with them.

"I'll do that," I say.

Somehow he is not satisfied with my answer. He remains standing there in my office. He asks the question again. "Will you take care of my family?"

Again, I tell him I will.

Again, he's not satisfied with my reply. He lingers. For a third time, he asks, "Charles, will you take care of my family?"

I finally get it. The promise I'm making is not a casual thing. I realize that if I don't do what I say I will, I will be condemned. On the other hand, if I don't make the promise, I'll be untrue to the person I want to be, the person the gods want me to become.

By now I know that I want to be someone who cares about others, without judgment. That's who Brother Honda in Hawaii wants me to be, right? Isn't that what Zion is all about? Isn't that also what Zen is pointing me toward? I want to overcome my personal weakness of withdrawing from others. I want to care about everyone.

After carefully thinking things through, I answer him again. This time I really mean it.

"Yes, Kerry. I promise. I promise you that I'll do my best to take care of Amy and the children."

Finally, he is satisfied with my answer and leaves. From that point forward, my life as a home teacher to the Dukes takes a new turn.

the master asked,
"lovest me more than these?"
nuthatches and warblers

I cannot give you all the details of what transpires over the years that follow. Many of those events are too personal and sacred to mention. What I can say is that nothing has taught me more about the truth of God's love than my visits as a home teacher to the Duke family.

I often think about why Kerry came to me. I wasn't his best friend. And I certainly was not the most righteous person around.

There had to be a different reason.

In the end, I can think of only one. He came to me because I was *assigned* to be his brother, his home teacher, his friend. That has to be it. Although many come to question the value of organized religion, and although some churchgoers don't take their responsibility to minister to others that seriously, the truth of the matter is that this calling to attend to the needs of others is far from trivial.

By way of service, we become God's arms and hands. We are the way he exists in the world.

Being a home teacher is as important as being a parent. Both roles help us learn how to extend ourselves to someone else. That is the essence of the gospel. Indeed, it is the essence of human existence. Involvement is our reason for being.

It is what I'm calling raking, pure and simple. We learn how to do what the gods want us to do, not what the "natural man" would do of his own accord. Again, we aren't smart enough to live without commandments. Without a little help, it doesn't occur to us to do the things that are necessary for our growth and for the salvation of others.

Brother Honda said it well. The measure of our righteousness is how we take care of the poor. Modernity has eroded our sense of compassion and belonging, so much so that we no longer live with a vibrant sense of our connection to each other. Say nothing, then, of our empathy for those among us who struggle because of their weaknesses or because of the way society directs opportunities to thrive away from them. We already know, as the cultural critics dutifully articulate, that we suffer from anomie, ennui, and solipsism. Too bad more of us don't actually listen for the answers to our questions about why life is not better than it is.

*

Over the years that follow, I do my best to be there for the Dukes. I give Amy and the children back-to-school blessings each fall. I bless them when they are sick and discouraged. When I do, the heavens open and very specific words of blessing and counsel come, as if Kerry is telling me what to tell them.

I fix the shower. I repair the clothes dryer. I pull out a shrub from the front yard with a chain tied to my pickup truck. I am there for many different moments of celebration and crisis—high school graduations, moments of doubt, times of sickness, occasions of triumph.

Life without Kerry is not easy for the Dukes. But every member of the family does his or her best to live a good life. Again, few things have been more inspiring to me than to witness how the Dukes have endured their trials.

*

One other thing I learn from the Dukes is that the divine power we feel (or don't feel) depends on faith. I've had the opportunity to give formal blessings to many different people over the years. I once thought that the effectiveness of these ministrations depended on my worthiness as the person giving the blessing. While that is not unimportant, what is *far* more crucial is the state of the person receiving help. Even a sinful person can deliver a dozen roses. But to have those flowers blossom in your heart, you have to believe that god loves you.

When someone sincerely believes they can receive a blessing from God, the power you feel when ministering to that person is noticeable. The conduit becomes wide, and the Spirit flows powerfully—usually from the earth, entering your legs and rising into your arms. What you impart to such people is not you, of course. It is God's power—a grounded and materially borne energy that fills the world and can, and should, be shared freely, generously, and carefully.

This sharing of God's energy is what we call love. It is a force that is amplified as it passes from one to the next—whether those involved are people, animals, trees, or stones.

Of all the things we can experience in this world, nothing compares to the feeling of helping others receive God's love. Of all the reasons not to sin, this is the one I find most compelling. Whatever the praises of the world, whatever the pleasures of the flesh, whatever relief we find in momentary distractions and indulgences, nothing compares to the simple joy that comes when we act out of compassion for the welfare of someone (or something) else. At this moment of eternal grounding, we are allowed to get a glimpse of the wonder of all things.

I believe this is the vision of Zion that Brother Honda wanted me to see, and I thank him for giving the same talk three times in a row.

*

Zen teaches a similar lesson. In contemplative moments of nothingness, the limits of the self fall away. We connect with everything and everyone when a lack of distinction becomes our lived reality. We are open, welcoming, available, receptive, aware. We are fair, nonjudgmental, and helpful. We are the sky, and not the passenger flying through it. We are the ocean, and not the tourist on the beach.

From evanescence comes dependent co-arising. All things influence each other. All things are influenced by other things.

Nothing exists in isolation. That being the case, we must try to live as well as we can, because the bad things we do affect everyone and everything in a negative way. Our bad deeds flow out into the world like waves radiating from a pebble dropped in a pond.

Attending to the garden teaches us that a breath of air is the sky. A leaf on a tree is the forest.

There are two things in this world we can't complain about—being stuck in traffic, and too many people in a crowd. We are that traffic. We are that crowd. Is there any other way to know traffic and crowds than to detest our being traffic and crowds?

This, I think, is the point of raking, the one I often missed completely. Life is high maintenance. Forget climbing to one! Just staying at zero requires constant vigilance and effort. Zero is enough. Zero is plenty. Zero is what there is to find, and to be.

Climb to two and someday you will fall to negative two.

Birds sing, and we hear them. Rain falls and becomes the sea. Trees make oxygen, and we breathe.

> lines in the sand—
> repeating the pattern that
> is never the same

We rake and rake. And then we rake some more.

Gradually, I have also come to understand that the garden of our souls can be a paradise. But this garden, east of Eden, will never be perfectly weeded, perfectly pruned, perfectly watered. As inhabitants of this "lone and dreary world," we will always fall short. We will always have weaknesses and will need to be forgiven for them.

The prophets have weaknesses, too. But this doesn't mean we shouldn't try to do what we can while we can.

There is no such thing as perfection. There is only raking the sand as well as we can. Each time is different. And the process that seems tedious and boring at first becomes exciting the more we do it.

Such is the calculus of our approach toward all that lies beyond earthly understanding. Rising up, we eventually return to the low. Surely, this is what Bashō meant by *kōgo kizoku* 高悟帰俗. We ascend to enlightenment, then return to the mundane. The measure of a person's highness is her lowness. Wisteria blossoms are prized because their gorgeous flowers bow low to the ground.

Here are two of my favorite poems from Bashō's *A Journey to the Far North*. They express *kōgo kizoku*.

> fleas and lice—
> a horse urinates
> near my pillow
>
> 蚤虱
> 馬が尿する
> 枕もと
>
> *nomi shirami*
> *uma ga pari suru*
> *makuramoto*
>
> how still!—
> the cry of cicadas
> penetrates the boulders
>
> 静かさや
> 岩にしみ入る
> 蝉の声
>
> *shizukasa ya*
> *iwa ni shimiiru*
> *semi no koe*

I am slowly beginning to reassemble the pieces of my shattered crystal ball. I'm learning how *not* to make progress. Just to stay on my feet. That's it. That's enough. Even that will be a miracle. Even that will be Lehi's experience of the tree of God's love. All I need is shade on a hot day, a drink of water when I'm thirsty, something to eat when my stomach growls.

That's all. That's plenty. Everything beyond our needs should be given to the poor. Why am I so selfish? So uncaring about others?

The storms come. My house never stays neat though I'm cleaning it constantly.

I learn slowly that there is much to learn about the few things that Jesus wants us to learn. The lessons never stop coming.

How much is there to learn? As my friend Kimberly Burnett puts it, "There is the 10% you know. The 20% you don't know. And the 70% you don't know you don't know."

I visit Walden Pond from time to time. I walk around the lake and think of Thoreau trying to become a fish. He loved white pines. The sacred cryptomeria at Heisenji are also tall and inspiring and dangerous.

CHAPTER 13

A Weedy Ditchbank,
An Enlightened Man

It is summer, and we are back on the farm. I lean my shovel against a barbed wire fence and squeeze between two strands to get through to the other side. Looking straight down, I see the warm-colored light of sundown passing through the leaves of the weeds directly below me.

I am struck by the beauty of the moment.

> enlightenment—
> I now have eyes to see
> the beauty of weeds

"This is a beautiful place," I say to my father, speaking about the desert valley that has become our home.

"Is it?" he responds.

Back in New England, I'm entering the Stop & Shop parking lot on Mass Ave in Arlington. I notice something shiny on the pavement.

The Rasmussen farm in Clarion, Utah.

I pull into a parking spot. I get out of the car.

The car next to me is parked in the opposite direction, back end in. The front window is down, and the driver, a man in his fifties, is sitting there, probably waiting for his wife while she shops.

To my surprise, I see that the entire length of his car is covered with a coating of oil and fish.

It seems that, when I pulled in, my front tire rolled over a can of sardines. That was the shiny thing I noticed on the pavement. The weight of my car squirted the contents of the can all over the man's car, and on him.

So he's sitting there with one arm out the window, fish on his forearm, shoulder, neck, and face.

I don't know what to say.

"I'm so sorry." I turn toward him directly. "Look what I've done."

I expect him to be angry. But he isn't. Not at all.

"Don't worry about it," he says.

"I'm so sorry," I say again.

I go into the store. My original thought was to pick up a few things. But I buy a lot more than originally planned because I'm hoping the man will be gone by the time I get back to my car.

I carry out four bags of groceries. I walk over to my car.

The car and the man are still there.

I notice that he's wiped the length of his car. The smashed sardines are gone, but you can still see the oil, glistening in the sun. He has cleaned himself up too. No more fish on his face or shirt.

I apologize again.

Again, he is calm and forgiving.

As I drive home, I vow to myself that someday I will be like that man—forgiving, at peace with the world, accepting of things that go wrong. My guess is that he's Irish Catholic. But whatever he is, he's obviously reached a level of enlightenment that I can only dream of attaining.

CHAPTER 14

Leif, Trout

WE STRUGGLE TO HAVE A SECOND CHILD. OUR FERTILITY specialist, Dr. Hill, seems confident about our chances. He shows us how to administer injections of progesterone. As he moves on to his next patient, he says, "Let me know if it's a boy or a girl."

We go home. We give it try.

Nine months later, it's a boy.

We name our second baby Leif. For us he is life.

> in his tight wrapper
> my son sleeps peacefully—
> the gray winter sky

Many years later, when I see Leif running across a lacrosse field or playing guitar with his friends, a familiar thought runs through my mind. "Leif is a miracle. Life is a miracle." While nothing is as normal as life, to my mind, normal things are God's greatest, most marvelous gifts.

The sun comes up. Water falls from the sky. Someone speaks, another understands. How is consciousness possible?

There is a place I like to visit in Utah. It is a small stream that sits on top of a mountain at about eleven thousand feet. No trails lead down the steep side of the ravine. No tracks of angler's boots show on the bank.

I come to pay my respects to this miraculous temple of bugs, fish, and water. Each encounter with the cutthroat trout that have survived here for millions of years makes me wonder. How can there be such life on top of a mountain surrounded by desert in every direction? How did the trout get there in the first place?

Using what I learned in the two geology classes I took at Stanford, I come up with a possible explanation. Millions of years ago, most of what we now call Utah was under water. Gradually, the land rose from a vast sea. The softer rock got eroded by the elements, but the harder flows of igneous rock provided a cap that protected certain layers of sandstone and limestone as they slowly climbed thousands of feet into the sky.

The fish rose with the rock. They took refuge in the streams that emerged from the receding ocean. As they were carried higher and higher toward the desert sun, the trout learned how to survive in the rain- and snow-fed waters that slowly carve away at the mountain. Through snow- and ice-bound winters, through the muddy spring runoff, through the dangerously low waters of summer and fall, the trout survive.

Who could not respect such animals and the world that has made their life possible?

*

I cast a small elk hair caddis toward the head of a pool. A splash. A tug. Fish on! I keep the largest male to feed my children, and quickly return the rest to the stream.

A cutthroat trout, Salina Canyon, Utah.

How devastating it would be to come to this water and discover that these wondrous trout, like so many of the earth's plants and animals, have died because of our carelessness and neglect. When will we be thankful for the things that sustain our lives?

> a secret stream—
> mayflies emerge from the rocks
> and turn into clouds

CHAPTER 15

Tufts, Divorce, More Home Teaching

AFTER TWO YEARS AT WESLEYAN, I DO A POSTDOC AT THE Reischauer Institute of Japanese Studies at Harvard. While back in Cambridge, I am hired by Tufts University to build a Japanese program. Tufts is located in Medford, a suburb of Boston, and we welcome the chance to move back to such an intellectually and culturally rich part of the world.

Starting a new program has its challenges. On the first day of class, I walk into my classroom to discover that I have one student. Over time, I gradually build up a clientele, and we hire two more professors. My students are not only brilliant, but they care about the world they are inheriting.

I work hard. I publish a few books. I get tenure.

*

I am asked to become the dean of the Colleges for Undergraduate Education. Now among the decision makers, I am shocked to feel the barbs of racial discrimination more sharply than ever before.

The person who hired me moves on to be the provost at another university. Without much support, I feel unwelcome. Rather than try harder, I retreat. Once again, my weakness of avoiding unpleasant situations gets in the way. A more aggressive person would fight back. But this world operates by rules I don't care for. As Professor Hibbett puts it to me, "I advised you. But I never advised you to become a dean."

This is not to say I don't learn many things as an administrator. One day, the astrophysicist Kenneth Lang comes to my office to talk about a certain matter. He brings me some of his books so I can get a feel for his scholarship.

I leaf through the heavy tomes. I try to show interest, not expecting to be able to comment on his work. But then, in one book I find a most unusual diagram. It's labeled "The heliosphere." It doesn't look like other diagrams of the solar system that I've seen before. It's not the usual big sun with small planets revolving around it. It looks more like a blob.

Professor Lang explains. "Most people think the earth revolves around the sun. But that's not technically true."

"It's not?"

"No. The earth revolves *within* the sun."

"I guess I don't understand."

He points to the diagram. "The sun's solar wind is a part of the sun. It creates a huge bubble in space called the heliosphere. The earth does revolve *around* the sun, but it always stays *within* the sun's radiation bubble. If that weren't true, we wouldn't be experiencing the light and warmth that we do. So in this sense we're revolving *in* the sun, not just *around* it."

Every now and then you meet someone who changes the way you see everything. For me, Professor Lang is one of these people.

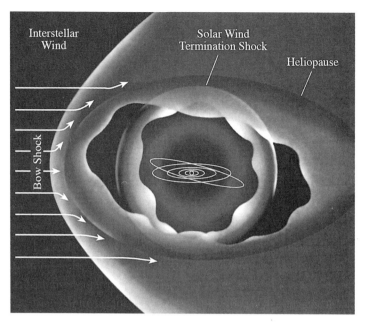

The Heliosphere. Courtesy of Kenneth Lang.

It is a change of prepositions: from *around* to *in*. The shift is seemingly small but profound. Moving from "The earth revolves around the sun" to "The earth revolves in the sun" changes how I view many other key relationships.

✳

There is a reason why prepositions are the parts of speech we master last when learning English. Nouns and verbs are relatively easy to understand. Tree. Rock. Grow. Walk. Even adjectives and adverbs are not so difficult. Fast. Red. Quietly. Quickly. But *around* and *in* are harder. Why? Probably because prepositions show relationship, and experience is required to know how one thing relates to another.

Which of the following is correct?

   a. I swam <u>over</u> the ocean.
   b. I swam <u>around</u> the ocean.
   c. I swam <u>in</u> the ocean.
   d. I swam <u>beneath</u> the ocean.

To understand which of these choices is correct, you have to know something about swimming (in its relationship to water). And the best way to know this is to find an ocean and swim.

To return to Professor Lang's diagram, the difference between the earth moving *around* the sun and *in* the sun is huge. My brief conversation with him not only changes how I think about the solar system, it also changes how I think about many other things, including my relationship with God, or the relationship between signs and the world, or the Buddhist concept of nothingness.

Once I think about it, Lang's diagram makes a lot of sense. Of course the earth revolves *in* the sun! What was I thinking? How could that not be the case? What did I think the sun was anyway, a big marble floating in the sky? I begin to wonder. Why do we so quickly move to separate a thing from its power or influence?

Of course the gods are not *way over there* while we are *way over here*. Of course the Creator of the world exists as the things of the world! If it is true that we sometimes live at a distance from "things," it is also true that at other times we lyrically merge with them. This would explain the presence of a disembodied ghost in the Godhead, the one of three who is different from the other two. Certainly, this anomaly encourages an involvement with God that we would otherwise think impossible. The Holy Ghost is to our heavenly parents as sunshine is to the sun. One cannot exist without the other. We experience the sacred below-the-line and also the sacred above-the-line.

It takes time to understand this relationship. Only certain kinds of immersive experience (made possible by a certain kind of awareness) reveal the truth of these things to us. As Paul put it so succinctly, spiritual matters are known spiritually.

Which of the following is correct?

a. God is <u>outside</u> the world.
b. God is <u>around</u> the world.
c. God is <u>beyond</u> the world.
d. God is <u>beneath</u> the world.

That's right. These statements are all false. Or should we say, rather, that they are all true misunderstandings? When thinking about the sacred, no one of these prepositions truly expresses the truth of our relationship to it. That's one reason the Buddhists call the state of enlightenment nothingness. Does "none" equal "no one?" Does "nothing" equal "no thing?" In a state of nothingness (*mu*), there are no barriers that prevent us from understanding anything else. There is no intelligent distance between things.

This is also true with "the Spirit of God like a fire is burning."

In the pursuit of the deepest truths available to our consciousness, a son is not separated from a father. A daughter is not separated from a mother. In Malachi we learn that the hearts of the children need to be turned to their parents, and the hearts of the parents need to be turned to the children. Otherwise, the purpose of the world is wasted.

One beautiful fall day in September 2001, the World Trade Center towers are struck by two hijacked passenger jets. The buildings burn and collapse. Many die.

As soon as I realize what has happened, I call Tufts Security. My immediate response as a dean is to make sure our Muslim student population is protected.

I drive over to the Muslim Student Center. For about an hour, I stand on the sidewalk, taking in the clear September afternoon while wondering what the future will bring. I look at my shadow and think about what my grandparents and parents went through after Pearl Harbor, when they were rounded up and sent to live in a concentration camp.

I can't predict the future. But I do know that Muslim students at Tufts will be blamed for things they did not do. Sadly, false judgment and overreaction will come. Hatred will weaken compassion. Calamity will be released upon the face of the earth.

Of course, it's silly to think that an attack on the Muslim Center should come that very afternoon. And it's absurd to think I could provide much protection if one did. On the other hand, how can the world's injustices mean anything to us unless we take them personally? So for an hour I stand on the sidewalk and stare at the street.

The sun-filled street, the sidewalk. They are a sign. *The* world is coming apart.

And if men come unto me I will show unto them their weakness. I give unto men weakness that they may be humble; and my grace is sufficient for all men that humble themselves before me; for if they humble themselves before me, and have faith in me, then will I make weak things become strong unto them. (Ether 12:27)

Despite my attempts to fix myself, some things don't change about me. I am making some progress. But I still struggle. I find myself sliding back into my old pattern of withdrawing from uncomfortable situations, including the many trying moments that marriage naturally brings. My farm-boy avoidance of people who challenge me is a real handicap in this realm of personal intimacy.

To put it in terms of changing prepositions, our slowness to master these words means that we are entering into new relationships over time that we don't yet understand. Of all the relationships we experience, marriage is perhaps the most delicate and demanding. Things in my marriage begin unraveling because I struggle to truly become one with my partner. I don't know how a husband truly positions himself in relation to a wife.

I never thought marital problems would come my way. Didn't my parents have a stable marriage? But problems come, and for good reasons. As much as I have learned about how to deal bravely with the world, in my personal life I still find myself avoiding difficulty.

My father has been worried about us since day one. "You two are so different," he says. And we are. I thought we shared enough to make things work. Yet thinking about "enough" is why we don't come to have "more." Only with great reluctance do I admit that our moments of silence are increasing and our unity is decreasing.

We seek the help of two different therapists. They are not very helpful.

My focus on "enough" makes me resist the idea of divorce. But gradually I come to see there is no other way out of the impasse we have come to. If marriage is not "more," then it really isn't marriage.

We get advice from a psychiatrist. He tells us to get everything worked out and only then to announce the details of our decision to our children, *fait accompli*. Involving them in the process will make them feel responsible for the outcome, and that would be damaging to them.

So the bad news is kept from Mie and Leif, and this new secrecy begins to hollow me out.

I am working in my study. It is early morning. My grandfather Inouye Sashichi appears. He is standing on my right. He comes to deliver a simple message. "This is a hard time for you. But just keep going. You're going to be fine."

As I think I mentioned earlier, my grandfather was my babysitter. For the first few years of my life, he and I did everything together.

We fed the pigs in the winter. We tended the garden in the summer. Our relationship was practically wordless, yet we understood each other pretty well, nevertheless.

During my freshman year, I jumped at the chance to learn Japanese. I remember coming home for winter break and greeting my grandfather in his language for the first time. "*Ojī-san, ogenki desu ka?*" ("How are you, Grandfather?") But he didn't answer. I tried again. I changed the words. "*Ohayō gozaimasu.*" ("Good morning.") Still no response.

Somehow, he refused to acknowledge that the little boy he once knew so well could now speak his language. I gave up. I was very disappointed.

Later, after my mission, when I started seriously looking into the details of his life, I learned something about him that surprised me. It turned out that my grandfather Inouye spoke English fluently! In fact, he was famous for his ability to do so. Apparently, he was the go-to guy for people in the Japanese-American community in the Bay Area. Whenever they needed to communicate with the *hakujin*, he was the one they looked to for help.

But then the War came. The US government sent him and his family to live in the horse stalls at Santa Anita, and he vowed never to speak English again.

So he didn't. At least not to me. The only thing I ever heard him say in English were a few different swear words.

*

All those years we lived together, we never did have a heart-to-heart talk. So this brief encounter with him in my study was the longest "conversation" the two of us ever had, and it happened after he had gone on to the next world. Maybe for that reason, the communication, though very simple, had a profound effect on me.

"This is a hard time for you. But just keep going. You're going to be fine."

Having faith and staying the course in hard times have proven to be the best way to deal with my troubles, whatever they are. My physical body, what I came to this world to receive, teaches me this same lesson. If we try to keep ourselves healthy, the various problems we have along the way clear up. Aided by the spirit, the body heals itself.

At some point, this stops being true, and the reality of life becomes death. But even old bodies heal themselves to a great extent.

Although my grandfather's visit is brief, I gain enough courage to deliver the bad news to Mie and Leif. We cry many tears. Never have I been this unhappy. Our family is a loaf of bread without salt, a peach that is not sweet.

David O. McKay's words, "No success can compensate for failure in the home," ring loudly in my ears. If anyone is a failure in this way, it's me.

> after many years—
> the pane of glass in the French door
> is still missing

I move out. My temporary home is a two-bedroom apartment on Tufts campus, 45 Winthrop Street in Medford. It's only a ten-minute walk from my office in Olin Center.

Many of my acquaintances avoid me. But my real friends step forward.

Paul Dredge and I still go fishing. Randy Petersen comes over and helps me fix up a room for Leif. Shelley Hoffmire buys me a rice cooker. Joan Sheahan, one of my home teachees, loans me some chairs so I'll have something to sit on.

*

I lug Joan's hardwood chairs up to my second-floor apartment. Otherwise, the place is empty and spotlessly clean. I put the chairs in a circle. I step back. I sit down on the shiny hardwood floor and stare at the chair Stonehenge from a distance. What am I going to do now?

> Without a table—
> the chairs have gathered to
> hold a conference

A little more about Joan, donor of chairs. She lives in a three-story house on Park Street in Arlington, just across from the water tower. When I home teach her, I usually sit on a stool in the kitchen. It's the only place where I *can* sit. All the other rooms are piled high with things.

Some months there isn't even a path to the kitchen, so I stand by the front door and give my lessons there while Joan sits on the bottom step of the stairway. The staircase to the second floor is covered with assorted objects—notebooks, calendars, spare batteries, flashlights, etc.

Joan's husband died soon after their divorce, so she raised three sons on her own. Although she came from a wealthy family in British Columbia, she has had to work hard to survive in Boston. Knowing how difficult it is for her to let go of anything, I am truly humbled by her gift of chairs.

CHAPTER 16

Rei Okamoto

I AM HOSTING AN ASSOCIATION FOR ASIAN STUDIES CONFERENCE at Tufts. Standing at the refreshment table at the reception, I meet a Japanese woman named Rei Okamoto. She has recently moved to Boston and is teaching at Northeastern University.

The moment I see her, something clicks.

I help her get settled into the community. I introduce her to the Reischauer Institute at Harvard. I invite her to the open house for the recently built Boston Temple, and she graciously attends. After the tour, she receives a copy of the Book of Mormon. She begins reading it and starts taking lessons from the missionaries.

Although she has not lived a religious life, she finds hope in what the missionaries teach her. She takes notes, writes down her questions. She studies and prays. She is what missionaries call a "golden" investigator.

Most importantly, she feels the Spirit, just as my mother did so many years ago at Charlotte's funeral in Sigurd. She accepts the missionaries' challenge to get baptized and asks me to baptize her. I witness new things come into her life, and that gives me hope.

I am taking a nap in my apartment. I now have a sofa and a table in addition to Joan's four chairs. It is late in the afternoon, about four o'clock. I wake up. Columns of sunlight enter from the windows on the west side. Standing about ten feet away is a young woman. Her hair is cut in a bob. She is twenty something.

Although we have never met, I immediately know who she is. She is no longer a girl of six—tied to that moment when the wind blew radioactive dust into our valley. I can hardly believe I'm meeting my sister Charlotte for the first time.

Like Kerry Duke and my grandfather, she also has a very specific message to deliver. Like the others, she wastes no time getting to the point.

"Charles, I know Rei. Go ahead and marry her."

I'm hesitant. My separation has not done great things for my confidence, and divorce proceedings are dragging on endlessly. And, of course, there is still the matter of my personal weakness—avoiding personal difficulty, retreating into my work.

But I also know that my sister Charlotte has come for an important reason. Encouraged by her visit, I know what I need to do. Most of all, I need to repent. I need to follow sorrow to where it *should* take me, not back to the world of judgment but ahead to the realm of compassion. I need to get over my weaknesses rather than just ignore them.

*

I introduce Rei to Paul. He was one of Dillon's friends at BYU and now works on his own as a consultant in Arlington. Beyond being my fishing buddy, he's someone whose opinion matters to me.

The three of us go to the Chatham "Tub" for striped bass. It starts to rain. Rei is wearing a leather jacket. By the time we walk back to the house where Paul is staying for the weekend, her coat is thoroughly soaked and probably ruined.

Rei says nothing about it, though. She remains calm. She seems happy to be spending time with me and Paul. Together, we enjoy the peace of Cape Cod. We have dinner together. Without having to say a word, I know that Paul thinks Rei is a good match for me.

My doubts slowly give way to hope for a new beginning. Doesn't Charlotte know Rei? Don't I believe in repentance and the ability to become a better person?

Rei grew up in Japan. After working as an editor for a few years, she came to the United States to get a master's degree in media studies. She stayed on and got her PhD, then landed a job at Oberlin College before coming to work at Northeastern. Many things about her remind me of my mother, and that helps me treat her with respect and warmth.

> hand in hand along
> the banks of the Charles—
> *kamo to kamo* (duck and duck)

June 12, 2004. Rei Okamoto and I are standing together in Annie's living room in Spanish Fork, Utah. Dwight, who is a bishop in one of the Gunnison wards, performs the ceremony. Annie prepares a dinner for all the guests, including Rei's father, who has come from Tokyo. Rei's mother, who passed away years ago, is present in the form of a photograph, which we place on the table next to us.

Melissa, my niece, makes the sherbet. Mie's other cousins help out. Dillon gives a generous talk about how everybody "including his dog" likes Charles.

*

After the dinner, I look out the window. Mie is sitting alone on the back patio, staring at the mountains in the distance.

I think about going to her. But I don't. Now is not the time.

I vow that I will make things better for Mie and Leif, who are deeply hurt because I divorced their mother. The first thing I need to do is to stay happily married this time. Whatever it takes. For them, and for me and Rei, I need to fix the things about me that keep getting in the way. Without God's help, I know I will fail again. That's the one thing I've learned from my divorce.

> the snow on Nebo
> has almost melted away—
> a June wedding

That evening, Annie breaks out the 70s costumes, and we have a disco dance. Sterling and Kif Adams, friends from my graduate school days in Cambridge, are there to help us celebrate the beginning of a new phase.

Sterling, who also loves to fly fish, dances a catch-and-release version of "Boogie Wonderland" by Earth, Wind & Fire. It's a very long song.

> dance *huu huu huu* dance
> Boogie Wondalaaa-aand—
> ha! ha! dance!

Rei's father returns to Japan. The day before we head back to Massachusetts, Leif begs me to get a dog.

"We don't have time for that," I tell him.

But Annie, who has recently found a mutt for her family, tells us where we can go online and check for shelter animals.

We give it a try. One site shows promise.

I talk on the phone with a woman named Barbie who has made it her life's mission to find homes for abandoned Labrador retriever puppies. She happens to have one available.

The next morning, we meet her at a park in Orem, just off I-15. She pulls up in a huge black Dodge Ram pickup.

Barbie's no nonsense. She drops the tailgate and produces a small black puppy from a portable kennel. She carries it over to where we're standing on the grass.

It's love at first sight. We play with the dog on the lawn. It's still early in the day, but it takes shelter in the circle of shade beneath Rei's skirt.

I can't believe we've found such a nice puppy. How can we be so lucky? My fortune is starting to turn.

The next day, we pack the car. We caravan with Warren's wife, Susan; my niece Melissa; and her husband, Joseph. Mie is staying for a few more days with her cousins and will fly back on her own. Leif is in the back seat with his new puppy.

The dog's name is Bridgett. Apparently, her former owners discovered their daughter has a severe allergy to dogs and had to give her up.

We think of renaming her Mei, but our niece Mei Li objects. We decide on Satsuki, which in classical Japanese means "the fifth month."

*

Satsuki has a gentle disposition. She tolerates the long days of driving well. She's so quiet we wonder if she knows how to bark.

We stop in Nauvoo, Illinois, to see the newly reconstructed temple and the jail in nearby Carthage, where Joseph Smith was killed. I take Satsuki for a walk in the parking lot in front of the motel. I pick up a twig and toss it out. "Fetch," I say, and Satsuki hops over to the stick and brings it back.

I'm impressed.

We return triumphantly to the motel room. "Hey, Satsuki's a born champ!"

Leif comes up to me. "Daddy, I have this thing on my neck."

"What thing? What are you talking about?"

I take a look. Sure enough, there are two large lumps on the side of Leif's neck.

"How long have these been here?"

Leif shakes his head.

I'm alarmed. I immediately call our pediatrician in Lexington. She instructs us to bring Leif in as soon as we get back to Massachusetts.

Is it some kind of tumor? I give Leif a blessing.

*

Rei and I attend a temple session in the newly rebuilt Nauvoo Temple. At one point, Nauvoo was the largest city in Illinois, even bigger than Chicago. It was a gathering place for the early members of the church before Joseph Smith was assassinated and everyone was driven out by mobs.

Thinking of Leif, I have a hard time paying attention to the temple ceremony, even as it unfolds before us with live actors playing the parts. My heart is filled with lead. But then, halfway through the endowment session, I receive a feeling of great peace. A burden is lifted from me as I receive the message that Leif is going to be fine. After the session, we walk back to our motel room. Not knowing what I will find, I discover that the bumps on Leif's neck are gone. I search for them, but they have disappeared. Maybe I was needlessly worried about some small thing. Still, I am humbled by God's power and compassion for me and my family.

*

We visit the Carthage Jail and the room where Joseph Smith was killed. Joseph was a man of both great strengths and great weaknesses. But the one thing about him was that he never denied the experiences that were given to him. I know that I, too, have my share of weaknesses. I also know that I need to be faithful in the same way. If I start denying the things I've experienced, then who am I?

I walk around the room and notice the window from which Joseph fell. I observe the thickness of the sill. I see for myself that it was not just the force of the bullets that blew him out of that room. He had to have come to the window so that others might be spared. Joseph Smith's last thought was to save others.

> how very wide!—
> the window sills at Carthage
> and the Mississippi

Kyoto, Family Reunion

I GET THE OPPORTUNITY TO DO RESEARCH IN KYOTO FOR A year. We leave Satsuki with Melissa and Joseph. Melissa is finishing up at Harvard, and Joseph is teaching middle school in Malden. Mie and Leif stay with their mother, who lives just four doors up the street on Massachusetts Avenue. They will join us for December break and again in the summer when school is out.

This is a particularly bad time to be away from Leif, who is transitioning into adulthood. But maybe he needs some time away from me in order to find himself.

Rei and I rent a small house in Katsura, down the hill from the International Research Center for Japanese Studies (Nichibunken). Rei makes me a *bentō* (box lunch) every morning before I bike up the hill to my office. About twice a week, she meets me at the Institute to play tennis with Suzuki Sadami, my advisor.

> September tennis—
> monkeys cheer us on from
> the wooded mountains

One evening, we lay our futon out on the tatami floor upstairs. We get ready to sleep. Reading in bed, I come to a passage in the Book of Mormon.

> Wherefore, . . . pray unto the Father with all the energy of heart, that ye may be filled with this love, which he hath bestowed upon all who are true followers of his Son, Jesus Christ; . . . that when he shall appear we shall be like him, for we shall see him as he is; that we may have this hope; that we may be purified even as he is pure. Amen." (Moroni 7:48)

I read the verse to Rei. "You know, I think I'm going to make that my goal this year—to see the face of Jesus."

We say our prayers and go to sleep. I assume it will take a while for my prayer to be answered. But that very night I have a dream.

In my dream I see Jesus. I'm surprised. He is not a white man. His complexion is much darker than in most of the images I've seen of him. He is neither smiling nor frowning. His eyes are dark brown. He has the look of a dedicated, highly intelligent person who is focused on a goal he wants to accomplish. And, yes, he does have long hair and a beard.

The image, burned into my mind, comes back to me many times over the next twenty-four hours. I see it superimposed on the faces of the people I meet—my fellow researchers at Nichibunken, the young women at the reception desk, the people shopping for groceries at the store near our house in Katsura.

> two thousand yen—
> the woman at the register
> looks a lot like God

By that evening, I finally understand the Zen of this image. The face of God is the face of everyone I meet. The gods are all around us. They are everywhere. There is nowhere that God is not.

Kyoto is home to three modest Latter-day Saint congregations. We begin attending the Nishi Kyōgoku Ward. Our first time there, we have a hard time finding the building. Turns out, it's little more than a rented warehouse with a small sign out front. There are only about thirty members.

I get called to be in the bishopric. By becoming intimately involved with this small group of people, I learn the importance of confidentiality and the role it plays in our spiritual growth. Learning about others is a necessary step in the expansion of the self that has to occur to anyone who would embrace the world with compassion. It is, in fact, the very foundation of trust, which, I have learned, is key to being "in the world, but not of it."

Trust. It comes down to this. What do we do with the knowledge we gain about other people? I believe this is the fundamental question of leadership and the ultimate test of our goodness and our ability to function as members of God's community. My personal weakness—namely, not becoming involved in the lives of others—is not really an option. Neither is complaining about the world's imperfections. On the other hand, deep involvement requires a great amount of concern and care.

Without the guidance of the Spirit, learning about others would only lead to betrayal and disappointment. Knowing someone's faults is one thing. Helping them get over them is quite another. What I learn, quite clearly, is that justice is not mercy. This is a lesson of love—one of the many miracles of raking in God's garden—that I'm learning slowly.

Mie and Leif come for the holidays. Rei's father also visits from Tokyo. We take them around to see our newly discovered favorite places, which include the West Mountain, where persimmons grow in great abundance.

I eat a persimmon every day and do not catch a cold that winter.

We get the chance to move to the Nishijin District of Kyoto. It's a much older part of the city. There are many important cultural sites near our house, even more than in Katsura.

We play volleyball on Wednesday nights with a group of Buddhist priests in training. They are all in their twenties, studying so they'll be able to assume leadership of the temples that their families own.

I want to ask them a question. I already know there's no such thing as a scriptural habit for Japanese people generally. That is, there is no established custom of constantly studying an authoritative text, one that tells people who they are and what their purpose is.

They are not like Muslims or Jews or Christians in this way. The *Heart Sutra* is a highly regarded text, for instance. But it is mainly copied and chanted, not read and explicated.

Could it really be true that Buddhist priests don't encourage their parishioners to study doctrine?

I am returning home from my office at Nichibunken. I spot my volleyball buddies in a small dive near the tracks. I pull my scooter over and go in. This might be a good time to ask them my question.

They offer me a seat and get me something to eat and to drink. As we talk about this and that, I wait for the right moment. In a lull in our conversation, I ask them, "I hear you don't encourage the members of your congregations to study the sutras on their own. Is that true?"

"That's right," they answer.

I explain to them how Latter-day Saints are encouraged to study doctrine on a daily basis. "Why don't you ask your people to do the same?"

They think for a minute. Obviously, no one has ever asked them this question before.

Finally, one of them speaks up, "Well, I guess we don't do that because it would confuse them."

"Confuse them." I repeat the words, which don't sink in immediately.

We visit for a while longer. Then I say goodbye and jump back on my scooter.

*

As I make my way home through the streets of Kyoto, I think about how study might lead to confusion. This runs counter to everything I've been taught up until now. But the more I think about it, the more I see their point.

In truth, there probably aren't many things more potentially confusing than studying the scriptures. How could I have not realized this before? More study does not guarantee more understanding and clarity. Didn't Paul say that the Greeks were "ever learning, and never able to come to a knowledge of the truth" (2 Timothy 3:7)? I've been making the assumption all along that reading, discussing, and writing are always good to do. But now I can see the many ways in which this is not actually true. Thomas Aquinas's study of Aristotle, like Alexander Kojève's study of Hegel, led to misunderstandings and confusions that the world has still not gotten over.

If anything, raking is a surer way to the kind of knowledge that matters most. The truth is something to practice, not something to think about.

> light truth hope knowledge
> virtue justice unity—
> *blah, blah, blah, blah, blah*

Paul and Nancy Dredge come and visit for a week. We make a point of visiting the Saihōji, the famous Moss Temple. After copying out the *Heart Sutra* with a brush and sumi ink—"Form is nothingness, and nothingness is form"—we tour the famous garden. Everything is covered with a thick layer of moss. It's been a while since we had a good rainstorm, so things are not at their most lustrous. But it's still impressively verdant.

Years later, I learn from my neighbor Helen Sussman that the key to growing moss is constant raking. Moss doesn't need fertilizer. Aluminum sulfate helps keep the soil acidic, and I apply that to my yard occasionally. But what moss wants most is a clear, stable, moist surface to grow on.

That's it! That's all! All moss needs is water and a place to grow. In a similar way, all compassion needs is some steady encouragement. Our capacity to grow in understanding will happen as long as we keep clearing a space for this to happen.

The spirit of Elijah turns the hearts of the children to their fathers, and the hearts of the fathers to their children. Rei and I plan a family reunion so our relatives in the United States can visit our ancestral home in Kyushu.

Including Mie and Leif, thirty family members show up in Kyoto. We ride the bullet train to Hakata. We board a chartered bus. After a stop in Dazaifu, we arrive at my grandfather Sashichi's village. It's a small place called Inaibaru.

We take turns praying before the family altar. This is the place my grandfather left in 1899. He went to Hawaii as an indentured slave to save the estate that was given to our family for service to their Lord Kuroda. Because of his sacrifice, the farm and the house are still here.

My cousin Inoue Hiroshi takes us to the family temple, the Honshōji 品照寺. He shows us the wooden locker that holds the pottery urn that contains the remains of our ancestors going back many generations.

I feel the presence of the dead as we cross the narrow valley where my grandparents once walked. Before us and behind us, the steeply rising mountains are covered with bamboo, cherry, cryptomeria, and ginkgo. The green is intense in the afternoon light. We watch hundreds of dragonflies skim back and forth above the drooping heads of rice.

*

That night, Hiroshi takes us to Amagi, where we visit the home of my grandmother Mikano. Unlike the Inouye farmhouse, this residence is dark and formal. Seeing its elaborate wooden panels—carved with turtle, crane, and plum blossom patterns—I begin to understand why Grandma Inouye was so driven.

We know that her first marriage ended, but we don't know why. Was it her husband's family or her own that was dissatisfied with the arrangement? We also know that she had to return to Amagi and that she was so hurt by her failed marriage that she began to decline. But, again, we don't have many details.

Then something unusual happened. Her cousin had made plans to travel to Hawaii with his wife, but she became pregnant and could not make the trip. So he had his parents ask Mikano's parents if Mikano could go as a proxy for his wife. Thinking a trip to somewhere else might help her recuperate from her depression, they agreed.

My grandmother was to be there for three weeks. But, while staying with family friends on the big island of Hawaii, she met my grandfather. They married and eventually moved to the West Coast.

They rented small plots of land in the Santa Clara Valley and grew strawberries and raspberries. They had four children—Helen, Mary, Charles, and Ruth. The plan was to work hard, save money, and eventually return to Japan. Having disobeyed her parents,

Mikano wanted to prove to them that she made the right decision by marrying my grandfather and that they had prospered in America.

But she never made it back to this dark, formal house. A month before their scheduled departure for Kobe, Mikano died of a heart attack. Perhaps that is why her spirit continued to haunt my father all his life. She was in his mind, telling him to work hard and to succeed, to be something more than his father had been. As the brother for whom his sisters sacrificed everything, he felt compelled to become a success.

*

We visit Mikano's relatives for an hour, then take our leave.

The sun has set. It's dark when we step outside.

We stand on the front porch of the grand house. Next to us is a glowing orb that has been set out for the Festival of Lanterns. It's there to help the spirits of the dead return home for their annual visit to the land of the living. Gazing at the lantern, I ask my cousin Jeanette, "Do you think Grandma comes back here for Obon? I mean, her family never really seemed to accept her for who she was."

Without hesitation Jeanette answers, "Oh, I think so. Home is home, Charles. We all have our disappointments. But we all want to be with our family."

The moment she says this, a dragonfly comes flying through the darkness. It lands with a *thud* on the lantern that glows between us. It rests there quietly, not a foot from our eyes. It lifts its head as if looking at us. I am speechless.

> a warm August night
> my grandmother returns home—
> now a dragonfly

Dragonfly. Courtesy of Hanne Hasu/Pixabay.

The gothic novelist and playwright Izumi Kyōka (1873–1939) wrote about dragonflies with skill and power. In his final work, "The Heartvine," dragonflies become women, and women dragonflies.

This remarkable story is about sorrow, death, and reconciliation. I think it's one of Kyōka's best, because here he acknowledges, just days before his death, the sacrifice others have had to make so he could live.

Kyōka depended on the compassion of women in particular. Both in his personal life and in his literary works, he required their giving. Perhaps this is why I am so drawn to his writing. Because I, too, have required similar sacrifices of my mother, my sister, and of the other women I have known. Like Kyōka, I have not always been thankful enough.

In my book on Kyōka, *The Similitude of Blossoms*, I wrote about a possible tie between his work and Jesus's death on the cross. It's an unusual thing to say, something no other scholar has even thought of saying. After all, Kyōka was an animist, not a Christian. He was also fond of saying that he was not influenced by the cultural forces of the West, unlike many of his contemporaries. But he did attend a missionary school for a short while, and powering the body of his work is an aesthetic need for bloody, compassionate sacrifice—though not by a man, but by a woman. Perhaps, while he was attending the missionary-run school, he saw an image of Jesus dying on the cross.

Something like repentance and forgiveness for a life of requiring the sacrifice of others appears in his very last story, "The Heartvine" (Rukōshinsō, 1939). This is a narrative about a seamstress who embroiders a handkerchief with a pattern of two dragonflies joined in flight, tip to tip. She is persecuted by her fellow seamstresses who accuse her of vulgarity. The real reason for their criticism, though, is their envy of her obvious talent. Filled with despair, she throws herself into the Kanazawa Castle moat, just as the male protagonist of the story is about to do the same. Apparently, this actual scene played itself out before Kyōka's eyes when he was a young man, about to commit suicide.

He revisits this memory in this last story. He is an old man, thinking back on that night when the young woman died, and he did not. The spirit of the dead seamstress returns as a dragonfly.

> See them
> 'neath a blade of grass,
> Waiting for
> The storm to pass.
>
> Hiding from
> Our prying eyes,
> Whitened silk
> and crimson dyes.

kyoto, family reunion

Two red leaves
on purest snow,
Wings erect
in love's sweet glow.

By lightning flash,
We see, we stare,
We fear and scorn
This tangled pair!

Oh, dragonflies
Stitched red on white,
Which one of you
Will die tonight?

CHAPTER 18

Saying Goodbye to
My Parents

We return to America and visit my aging parents in Gunnison. My father is in his late eighties. He's still working, though recently he has had a few operations to remove a blood clot from his head. My siblings think he fell off a ladder, but we can't be sure.

One afternoon, he asks me if I could give him a hand. As always, I say, "Sure."

My work clothes are still in the drawer in the basement bedroom where I left them.

I get dressed and climb into the pickup. Once again, I am submitting my will to his.

It usually takes us ten minutes to drive out to the farm, just enough time for a short conversation about international politics or some such topic. But this time we're in motion for less than half a minute. The truck travels only about eighty yards and stops.

My father turns off the engine. He slowly opens his door and steps out. He gets a hoe from the back and begins weeding the side of the road. I'm expected to do the same.

"This isn't the farm," I want to say to him. "Why are we working here?"

But I don't say anything.

I look for another hoe.

As I join my father on the roadside, I think I finally understand something that has taken me a lifetime to learn.

All these years my father has been asking me to help him on the farm, and all these years I've been giving up my freedom to please him, to be loyal to him. Only now do I finally realize that he wasn't really asking me to work *for* him. Rather, he was asking me to be *with* him.

Once again, it's a matter of getting the prepositions right.

Finally, it all makes sense. Didn't my mother once tell me that my father liked company when he worked? "Someone being there at his side makes him happy," she used to say.

Like me, my father is a lonely man. I was with him when I fell onto the hay mower. I was with him when his foot got caught in the ditcher. All those years of my childhood and youth, working on the farm every day, weeding beets, driving tractor, sorting potatoes. Until I was forty, I returned each summer to help him.

For him, I was the cricket, chirping outside his window. And then I disappeared, leaving him to the silence of the Utah wind.

I wasn't with him when he slipped from that ladder and hit his head. It should have been me, climbing up to inspect the seed cleaner, not my father. It should have been me who fell. I would have survived without injury. That's how life is supposed to be.

✻

While we cut down the weeds on the roadside, I think about those lonely years when my father worked by himself, with none of his sons to help him. For that final stretch, he must have felt abandoned, with no one at his side.

For the best of reasons—to live my own life—I left him, just as I left Mie and Leif for those months we were in Kyoto. Noguchi-sensei would have done the same. Professor Hibbett probably would have done the same. But if there's one thing I deeply regret, it's not being there for my father, or for my children, when they needed me.

The afternoon sun beats down. My hoe glances off the hard surface of the roadside. I secretly shed a tear or two, wishing I had been a better son and father.

> the plan of happiness—
> grandfather dies, father dies
> son dies

> the plan of happiness—
> grandmother dies, mother dies
> daughter dies

> who's helping whom?—
> the sharp edges of steel hoes
> scratch the gravel road

My relationship with my Heavenly Father is much the same. I am not supposed to be raking *for* him. Rather, I am supposed to be raking *with* him.

All we who live east of Eden, as we wander away from the burning house, the question is not "Where is God?" The question has always been, "Where are you?"

The weather turns cold. Frost kills the flowers in my mother's garden. Another growing season is over.

Now that everyone is back home in America, my mother decides to leave us. She stops eating in the morning. By evening, she's weak and beginning to fail.

Around noon the next day, a nurse enters the kitchen and tells everyone to come quickly. We get up from our chairs and go to my mother's bedroom. We find her struggling for breath.

We gather around. I sit on her bed and hold her in my arms. I hear a last sigh, and then I feel, five seconds later, the life leaving her body.

> frosted chrysanthemums—
> my mother's final breath
> and then one more

The woman who was once so strong and vibrant, the wife who was so loyal to my father, the mother who loved us all, is gone.

> no more back scratches—
> the cold September frost spreads
> over the front lawn

People from the mortuary come. We put my mother's body on a gurney and place a white sheet over her. We begin wheeling her to the front door. But then we remember something.

"We should give them to Annie," Dwight says.

Everyone agrees.

We fold back the sheet. We remove the rings from my mother's fingers, then pull the sheet back over her.

The way we handle the white cloth reminds me of a movement I've seen before. The muscles of my arms and hands remember it. But when and where?

Then I realize.

It's the sacrament ordinance I'm recalling. The offering of the body and blood of Jesus. Each Sunday, we fold the white cloth back, pass the bread and water, then cover the emptied trays with the cloth again.

I never thought of the white sacrament linen as a covering we put over his dead body. Now that my mother has taught me this point—this final lesson about Jesus—I can't take the sacrament without thinking of her life of sacrifice and how she would always say, "A thankful heart is a happy heart."

Now, when I'm asked to bless the emblems of Jesus's death and to tear the slices of bread into pieces with my hands, my sorrow is almost overwhelming. I don't want to do it. But someone has to do the breaking and the pouring so his body and blood can be shared.

> proof that God lives—
> listen, during the prayer
> the babies are quiet!

Taking the sacrament is a part of the raking we do every week as a remembrance of the day we were made clean. We remember. We give "the self" away. We share a name and an identity. We promise, again, to keep God's commandments so that the Spirit will be with us in Zion's nothingness.

✳

My father lasts only another month. He has no desire to live now that the woman he loved is gone.

Mie, Leif, and their cousins take turns caring for him during his final days.

Shortly before he leaves us, he makes a point of saying to me, "Charlie, I used to feel cursed and forgotten. But now I can see that the hand of God led us, our family, out of California to Utah."

The bitter man who said he believed in ideas, not in people, came to trust his cookie-baking neighbors and their kind gods.

They, both the gods and the neighbors, learned to call him by his name. They loved him and his family.

I'm not saying that ideas are unimportant. But the ones that matter most are embodied by the people who anchor them in the world of things.

We bury him next to my mother, in the foothills of Salt Lake City. Charlotte is a few feet away. Her remains have been moved from Richfield. This is greener place than down south, but it doesn't really feel much like home to me. I have spent my entire life being critical of this city and its Cartesian modernity.

I would rather end up by some cedar tree or clump of sagebrush in Sanpete County or on Tufts campus next to the ginkgo tree whose ancestor survived the atomic bombing of Hiroshima. We brought the sapling from Japan and planted it there, as a testament to forgiveness and peace.

> the journey from Ur—
> this dust is not my dust
> this earth is not home

> death by diarrhea—
> oh, how painful was the morning
> when Siddhartha died

With my grandparents and parents gone, I feel a new loneliness. I want nothing more than to see them again someday. I want the story of family happiness to be true, to be real. Death, I hope, will be a happy reunion. Death, I hope, will be the big happiness that exists above the line, one step higher than romance and marriage and family.

death (eternal life)
marriage
romance

———————————

sexual union
eating/drinking
life

Figure 1. Physics and metaphysics. Above the line exists the world of ideas. Below the line resides the world of things.

Faith or not, death or not, it is hard for anyone to live without parents and grandparents. Sometimes I feel my people close by, as if they are the air around me and in the earth beneath my feet. Annie tells me she knows they are looking out for the safety of our children—saving them from traffic accidents and worse.

Although I desperately want to see the dead again, I receive no more visits from the other side. I guess I shouldn't want or need such miracles. In the first place, they never happened because I asked for them.

above the desert—
the high cumulus clouds
move by in straight rows

I burn incense before our family altar and watch the tendrils of smoke rise peacefully toward the heavens. The number of people to remember grows steadily larger year by year.

tangerines and rice—
smoky strands of DNA
curl toward the ceiling

CHAPTER 19

The Longfellow Park First Ward

I AM CALLED TO BE IN ANOTHER BISHOPRIC. I'M HAPPY TO do what I can to help God's love reach his children in need. The Longfellow Park First Ward meets across from Henry Wadsworth Longfellow's former house on Brattle Street in Cambridge. It's a congregation for young single adults.

I am a counselor to Ken Hafen, a man I have never met before. He's originally from Provo, Utah. His father was a professor at BYU. He tells me, "All my dad ever did was work—work work and church work."

Ken reminds me of my Gunnison friends. He is honest in the same way. Ken told me that he wanted to get married right out of high school. When he asked for his father's blessing and didn't get it, he and Tammy got married anyway.

I can see why. Tammy is a remarkable, loving person. Like Ken, she is both gentle and strong. She keeps their home filled with flowers, children, and grandchildren. Maybe I'll get my act together and have a marriage like the Hafens' someday.

*

Bishop Hafen asks me to see what I can do to help the sisters. He has me attend Relief Society, a meeting that is usually for women only. For the next three years, I have this rare window into the souls of fifty or so women in their twenties and early thirties. I experience many unforgettable things.

*

I am walking up the stairs in the Longfellow Park chapel. I am to set one of the sisters apart for a calling she has accepted. A voice whispers to me, "Make sure she knows of the blessings I have in store for her."

We talk for a few minutes. I place my hands on her head. I set her apart for the calling. Then I add a few words. "Our Heavenly Father wants you to know that you can have any blessing you want from his hand."

She breaks down in tears.

I am deeply moved by her faith and sincerity.

*

This sort of thing happens again and again during my time in LP1. I learn that few things make me happier than giving blessings to others. When this happens, I am but a mouthpiece. At best, I am a jar for the jam, and certainly not the source of God's sweetness. Even so, to be a small part of the process, to feel a divine love coursing through me on its way to another person is an astounding, moving experience.

*

One morning, the women in the room all stand. They sing a song they learned when they were young girls in Primary. It seems they remember every word. I am impressed with this impromptu chorus. Remarkably, they still seem to have the simple faith they had as children.

These are those who are still enduring to the end. Many have fallen away because of their choices and because of disappointment. For some, their dreams of marrying and raising a family will come true. For some, it won't, at least not in this life, or not as imagined.

But I know there are blessings for all those who remain faithful. No matter what comes, good or bad. The truth is that we are blessed immeasurably if we learn how to share our lives with others. We can't control who or what comes our way, and we all come with various weaknesses to turn into strengths. But we do have a say in how we understand our experience of the world.

✻

I get a call from one of the sisters. Apparently, evil spirits have infiltrated her house in Jamaica Plain. She hears ghosts talking.

I drive over there with Rei. We visit for a while. I give her a blessing of comfort.

We're about to leave when she asks me, "Brother Inouye, what should I do if it happens again?"

The temple ceremony comes to mind. I ask her if she remembers the scene where Lucifer tries to interfere, and Peter tells him to get lost. "Remember that part?"

"I do."

"So how about telling your ghosts to leave? But don't forget to say 'in the name of Jesus Christ.'"

She nods. We leave.

She never has that problem again.

✻

As the temple teaches us, evil has no power over those who have faith. While it's important to acknowledge Satan's influence, we don't have to put up with his nonsense, or with the promptings of the unembodied third that fell away with him in the premortal existence. To put it bluntly, they are a bunch of losers. Having some level of compassion, even for them, is one of the most effective ways to combat evil.

Evil is surprisingly simple. Satan has no body. He and his followers only have the pretend legs, arms, mouths, and eyes that we give them. They like to make-believe they are us. But there is not much to be gained by our believing we are them. They have no drink or food to give us, certainly no fruit or cookies.

> seething with envy—
> the dancing bears of Satan
> have no hips or lips

About two years into my calling, I jokingly tell the sisters, "Thanks for letting me attend Relief Society with you. You're helping me discover my feminine side. I'm a lot more competitive than I used to be."

Amber Hardy laughs. But many of the others don't.

One beautiful afternoon in May, the church on Brattle Street burns down. Ken and I begin looking for a place where our congregation might meet. We find a temporary home in the Episcopal church just across the street. Reconstruction of the Longfellow Park chapel begins right away.

CHAPTER 20

Matt, Kan, Marc

Back in the Arlington Ward, Kimberly's husband, Matt, tries to fight the cancer in his body. He holds on for a number of years. He has a hard time understanding why he has to say goodbye to his wife and two sons. Toward the end, though, he finds peace and stays around long enough for his family to come to accept this tragedy that threatens to crush them.

When I visit him to say goodbye, his face is glowing with peace. He's ready to go. He's finally received an assurance that Kimberly, Ian, and Collin will be able to understand why he has to leave them. Pale and gaunt, he enumerates his many blessings, including his beautiful family and his affordable house in Arlington. A few days later, this once vigorous man who loved basketball, fly fishing, and motorcycling passes on.

Rei and I dream of having children even though we've gotten off to a late start. We try various infertility treatments. They are expensive;

and none of them work, including a generous gift of donated eggs from my niece Aimee Takasaki, Annie's daughter.

We decide to try to adopt a child through LDS Family Services. There are many forms to fill out. Not only that, but over eight hundred couples have already finished an application and are waiting for a baby. We go online to see their profiles. Their postings are filled with photos of smiling young couples wearing cardigans and standing in groves of trees. We are older than them all. It's hard to see why we would be chosen.

Informational meetings, interviews, and home visits follow. A year passes, and we still haven't written the letter to the birth mother. It's the most important part of the application because it explains who we are and what kind of life her child would have if we were the parents.

We get a call from Annie. She has some experience in this matter since she's adopted three children of her own—Stephen, Aimee, and David. She also has a friend, Sally Lee, who works for LDS Family Services in Honolulu. Sally has mentioned to Annie that one of her acquaintances has a daughter who is planning to put her baby up for adoption. If we're planning to adopt, now would be a good time to finish our application. There's no guarantee we will be chosen, of course.

Rei and I finally write the letter. It doesn't go well for three reasons. First, Japanese people aren't fond of talking about their virtues. Second, it's hard to write a personal letter to someone you don't know. Third, there's the faith issue. Do we really believe we will be chosen over eight hundred other families? The odds are not in our favor.

What we finally come up with is short and perfunctory, especially my half of it. My letter begins rather hopelessly: "To be perfectly honest with you, I sometimes wonder if I'm still young enough to raise another child." By contrast, Rei's letter is heartfelt and positive. "I love my husband. I feel so blessed to be able to live my life with him."

*

We attach a few photos and send everything off. The initial reaction is not good. Sally reads our letters and tells Annie that they're "a little short."

*

A week passes. I'm working at the Boston Temple. I've been assigned to sit at the front desk. I'm new to this work and eager to get some practice memorizing the scripts. I would rather be helping patrons who have come to do ordinances. But front desk it is.

As I expect, not much happens. A few people come in. I check their recommends and welcome them to the temple. In my spare time, I begin reading the copy of the Book of Mormon that happens to be on the shelf behind the counter.

I randomly open up to the second book of Nephi, chapter two. I read the line "to act and not to be acted upon" and am struck with a great force. Never have written words made a stronger impression on me. "To act and not to be acted upon" is about the freedom we have because of the Atonement. To me, though, it has an additional meaning.

If Rei and I are going to have a chance to get that baby in Hawaii, we need to "act and not be acted upon." We need to live with real faith, with an unwavering sense of purpose.

The next day, unable to forget the words I read the night before, I decide not to go to work. I sit down at the kitchen table and begin writing another letter. "Dear Birth Parents, thank you for considering our family. Here are some brief answers to some of the questions you might have about us."

I do not stop to eat or drink or rest. This time, it's as if I can see the birth mother in my mind. I write directly to *her*. With the Spirit guiding me, I describe our family and what life would be like for her child, should he or she come to our home. Fourteen questions and three carefully worded single-spaced pages later, it's four in the afternoon.

I'm dripping with sweat. Because time is of the essence, I immediately send the letter to Hawaii as an email attachment.

> running out of time—
> green bugs quietly chew on
> the dwarf maple tree

A few days pass. No word. We wonder if the birth mother has chosen another family. We cling to the slight chance that she might change her mind.

That night, I dream about a baby in a car seat.

Morning comes. We sit down for breakfast. I tell Rei about the dream, and I allow myself to get my hopes up by saying, "You know, I think we might get that baby after all."

We say our usual morning prayer and add, "Father, we thank thee for all we have. If it is thy will, we pray for that baby to come to our home."

Not more than ten minutes later, the phone rings. Rei picks it up.

It's the woman from Connecticut, the one who works for LDS Family Services. She was the one who came to our home to interview us a few months ago.

"Yes. We're sitting down. Yes. Charles is right here."

I try to piece together the conversation between Rei and the social worker. It's just what we want to hear. There's a young woman in Honolulu who has chosen us to be the parents of her baby. Hallelujah!

*

About a month later, we're in Hawaii. Abe and Sally Lee have offered to put us up at their home in Manoa Valley. Sitting on the back porch, gazing at the tree line on the crest of the surrounding mountains, we wait for the baby to arrive.

The child is overdue. We continue to pass the time by correcting term papers and final exams. We visit our relatives in Honolulu—Martha Fujimoto and her family and Edna Yonaoshi and her family.

We wait and wait. Still no baby.

Rei stays at the Lees' home, but I'm restless. I go surfing with Abe.

I help Sally harvest bananas in her backyard.

I help out with a luau at the home of one of the members of the Lees' ward.

*

Finally, the big day comes. It's a boy, or so we're told. Two days later, Sally brings him to us from the hospital. We're standing in the living room when she carries him in.

> Huli huli chicken!—
> our baby is delivered
> in a blue car seat

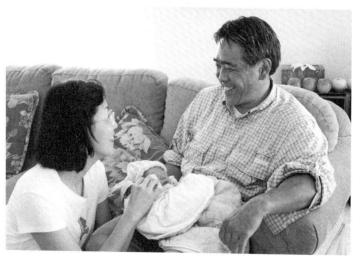

Rei and I meet Kan for the first time. Honolulu, Hawaii, 2010.

A few days later, we meet the birth parents. They come over to the Lees' for lunch. We have a nice visit. They are handsome, intelligent people.

Needless to say, we're grateful to them for having the baby. These days, most young mothers would have terminated the pregnancy, unwilling to accept the considerable difficulties and the cost associated with bringing a new life into this world. But, being supported by her family and knowing God's love, she did everything she could to save the baby, with the result that many wonderful blessings follow. I wonder if young women who unexpectedly get pregnant realize how many families are waiting for the opportunity to raise a child.

*

The birth mother tells Rei and me that our second letter made her change her mind about us. In other words, had I not read those words in the Boston Temple, "to act and not to be acted upon," we would not have received this blessing of another child.

We name him Kan, 寛, which means "generous." God is generous. Kan's birth parents are generous. Annie is generous. Sally Lee is generous. The only word for this great blessing is *kan*.

We hope that Kan will be generous too. We hope he will live up to this name—though, of course, his fate is his to choose.

By law, there is a time given to the birth mother to change her mind if she so chooses. We wait another week for the grace period to end. She doesn't waver. We fly back to Boston a threesome.

When we get back to Lexington, Mie and Leif greet Kan with open arms. They are a loving big sister and brother. Our dog Satsuki, though, is another story. She has been the baby of the family for the past six years and is more than a little jealous.

"Hey. What's going on here?"

It takes a while before the two become friends.

> sniffing the car seat—
> a newborn baby and a
> middle-aged dog

A few months later, we take Kan to the Cambridge courthouse for the necessary legal procedures. On the way home, we have pancakes at our favorite diner on Boston Avenue in Medford.

Not long after that, Kan is sealed to our family in the Boston temple. Annie flies out for the day. She's here to carry Kan into the sealing room. When the two enter, he's dressed in white—white shirt, white pants, and white socks with no shoes. Annie sets him on top of the altar. Rei and I join hands, and Annie puts Kan's little hand on top of ours.

A sealing is performed. We are bound together in what we Latter-day Saints call "the new and everlasting covenant." This joining of people one to another is what Shinkai Makoto, the director of the animated film *Your Name*, would call *musubi*, connection 結び. The idea is simple and powerful. Even death cannot break the bonds between those who love each other. Those bonds, like love and like life itself, continue forever.

During Kan's first three years of life, the three of us—Satsuki, Kan, and I—spend many hours exploring the Lexington woods.

> along the path—
> my young son and my old dog fight
> over the same stick

Not unlike Kan, I, too, am learning how to walk. Step by step, I'm trying to walk the path that the gods have set out before us. We live by faith. We seek for things we hope for but don't really understand. We make covenants. They are the Way.

Kan in the New England woods.

Gradually, I am learning how to care for the world. Every day, I pick up my rake and go out into the garden. I work hard in order to maintain my promises to the world.

With God's help and with constant effort, we can come to the one heart and mind of Zion. We can build a world in which there are no rich and poor. But to do that, we must understand that the Atonement is an *unearned* gift to all. As the O'Jays put it, "Get on the love train! You don't need no ticket."

As Kan grows stronger, others grow weaker. Marc Butler, a long-time member of the ward, becomes seriously ill. I go to see him with Jim Johnston, a good friend and member of the Arlington Ward.

Marc's wife, Deb, and his son, Sam, are in the room. It is a bright afternoon. The sunlight pours in through the plate glass windows of the Kaplan House in Danvers.

Marc is no longer responsive. He has not spoken for days.

We know that Marc loves music, so Jim and I decide to sing "Brightly Beams Our Father's Mercy," the Arlington Ward's unofficial theme song.

> Brightly beams our Father's mercy
> From his lighthouse evermore,
> But to us he gives the keeping
> Of the lights along the shore.
>
> Let the lower lights be burning;
> Send your gleam across the wave.
> Some poor fainting, struggling seaman
> You may rescue, you may save.
>
> Trim your feeble lamp, my brother;
> Some poor sailor, tempest tossed,
> Trying now to make the harbor,
> In the darkness may be lost.[1]

God's light is the higher, brighter one. It radiates from atop the lighthouse and is easily seen by all. To someone struggling to get to shore, though, the lower lights, the feeble lamps of people like

193

you and me, are also needed. Without this secondary light, this dim and flickering spirit of fallible people, the "fainting, struggling seaman" will not make it past the rocks and currents that block the way.

As we sing, a quiet sound comes from Marc's bed. He does not move. His eyes remain closed. Yet from his lips comes a low and contented humming as Marc provides the bass line for our humble choir. The next day, he crosses to the other side.

From this experience I realize something I sensed all along: in its direct engagement with our consciousness, music can open our hearts to God's love and lead us to a sharper understanding of his purposes. Music is one of the arts of nothingness.

*

As I gradually learn how to live more intuitively, I become increasingly aware of death's constant presence. We go to Crane's Beach in Ipswich for the Arlington Ward's annual clambake. I'm helping out with the cooking of lobsters, clams, corn, and hot dogs. The person in charge asks me to offer a blessing on the food. As I pray, I feel moved to ask specifically that our children be protected while "in the water and on the shore."

After lunch, we are all on the beach, enjoying the last warmth of summer. The long New England winter is not far away. A thunderstorm quickly moves in from the southwest. Everyone runs for shelter as lightning strikes and thunder cracks. I'm one of the last to leave.

I'm hurriedly loading tables and gas burners onto my truck in the pouring rain. I look up to see a group of lifeguards bring two bodies up from the beach.

One of them, a brown-haired woman, is facing our way. She is motionless. Her eyes are closed. Her mouth is open. Her chest exposed.

Both people are rushed to a nearby hospital.

Over the next few days, I keep scanning the papers and listening to the radio. I learn that the women were close friends, swimming in the water together, just offshore from where our group was playing in the sand. When we saw the clouds coming our way, we were able to escape to safety. But the two women, unaware of the approaching storm, were struck by lightning while still in the water. One was resuscitated at Beverly Hospital. The other didn't make it.

I mourn for the two friends, suddenly separated.

> swimming together
> along the shore at Crane's Beach—
> lightning and thunder

Note

1. Philip Paul Bliss, "Brightly Beams Our Father's Mercy," in *Hymns* (Salt Lake City: The Church of Jesus Christ of Latter-day Saints, 1985), no. 335.

CHAPTER 21

A Dream about Kan,
Some Thoughts on Faith

KAN IS A BEAUTIFUL CHILD. AS WE WATCH HIM GROW, REI and I are constantly reminded of God's love for us all. That love is one constant *kata* in a world of all things always changing. As Bashō would say, *fueki ryūkō*, there exists the unchanging even within constant change. Good poetry is written at those moments when we perceive the constant forms that exist within this ever-changing reality, when moments of truth make a mark on our trembling hearts and minds.

Like Mie and Leif, Kan has come to earth to be in our family. We belong to each other for specific reasons. Those reasons are not always clear. They have become obscured by the veil of forgetfulness that separates mortality from when we once lived with our heavenly parents. Over the span of a well-lived lifetime, though, those reasons can slowly become obvious. *Fueki ryūkō*. We consider the times and the people who touched us the most. As we continue to rake the sand in our garden, the patterns appear.

✳

I discuss this idea with the Johnstons, with Jim and his wife, Mary. She laments that, despite their best efforts, most of their children are no longer active members of the Church. "We don't understand what happened," she says.

"But isn't that why they're your children?" I suggest an answer.

They are puzzled.

I explain. "One thing I've noticed about your family is how different your children are from one another. They each have very distinct personalities. They each have chosen a distinctive path. That can only mean you raised them in a way that allowed them to be themselves."

"Maybe so."

"So don't you see? They chose you to be their parents because they knew you would love them for who they are. And you do, right?"

"Yes. Of course."

If we were to judge parents solely by how their children "turn out," then wouldn't our heavenly parents be the worst father and mother of all? They are the parents of both Cain and Abel, of both Nephi and Laman. But we never think of them as bad parents, and this for two reasons. First of all, we come to learn that God's love is for everyone, regardless of who they are. God's love is the rain that falls on the just and on the unjust. It is the milk and honey bought without price. And it is the love train for which "you don't need no ticket."

Secondly, we learn that we have the freedom to choose that love for ourselves. We either get on the train or we don't. No one can get on for us.

I have a dream. I see a room filled with scraps of white paper. Something scurries beneath the layer. It runs this way and that. Paper flies into the air.

It's a lobster. It's a crab.

Let's say it's a "lobster crab."

I open the door. The creature leaves the room.

I follow it outside. The lobster crab turns into my young son Kan.

There he stands in the gently falling snow, wearing his dark blue hooded coat, gloves, and rubber boots. He is looking at the ground around his feet.

"What are you waiting for, Kan?" I force myself to ask the "father" question.

The snow continues to fall. I count the white flakes as they fall from heaven and melt on his cheeks and eyelashes.

"Kan, that way is the fresh water. And that way is the ocean."

He nods. He turns toward the ocean and slowly starts walking away.

> a snowy day—
> an old man dreams of storms
> that must come and go

I wake up crying. The vision is cryptic, but I know exactly what it means.

In order for Kan to fulfill his mission here on earth, he will have to strike out on his own. Like Siddhartha, he will have to leave the safety of home. Like Adam and Eve, he will have to be expelled from the garden. Where will he go? And when? He has a choice— fresh water or salt.

I say it is a choice. But because he's a lobster crab, he knows that he's meant for the ocean. That is his nature. That is his calling. Even so, he still has to choose his nature for himself. That is the choice given to us all.

If he leaves home, will he come back here, to this place where we begin and end? Will I be here to witness his return? As his sixty-something father, I am proud to see him move closer to his fate, a little more each day. And yet, a father and a mother worry just the same.

Is it because I'm Japanese? People don't expect me to be a Latter-day Saint. I am attending a dinner at the Harvard Faculty Club. One of my colleagues speaks openly about the foolishness of people who believe in god. He doesn't know that I'm a believer. And I don't volunteer that information because I'm genuinely interested in what he has to say.

My question to him is pretty simple. Why do we not believe? Why turn that part of our minds off? If someone can sing, what does he or she gain by not singing?

Truly, many of his questions are my questions. His misgivings are my own. I understand that horrible things are done by religious people. Many profit off others, claiming to know God's will. Many turn to violence in the name of Elohim, Jesus, and Allah. Although they are meant to be sources of forgiveness and compassion, they are ascribed to be sources of hatred and fear.

I get all that.

But living without faith is no way to fix the countless problems that continue to plague us, even in the wake of Reason and Enlightenment.

In the end, rational self-interest and goodwill for all are not the same thing. The limits of human intelligence, which we find in the uneducated and the educated, are obvious and heartbreaking. Were it not for the reality of inspiration and godliness, I might very well feel compelled to give my allegiance to positivism. But the truth is this. The love of God is abundantly given to anyone who has the mind to perceive it.

If we have the capacity to have faith, we are also capable of real doubt. Fair enough. I know this too. If there is a decisive difference between me and my atheist colleagues, though, it is that I have come to understand that doubting, too, is a divine gift, a path to understanding what is real and what is not.

The doubt that leads to happiness must be as godly as the will to accept divine inspiration. As Paul puts it, what but the Spirit allows us to understand the things of the Spirit?

I remember writing to Dennis Rasmussen while on my mission. It was a calm winter day. You could almost count the snowflakes falling through the Sapporo sky. Frustrated by how few people seemed to be responding to the message we missionaries had to offer, I asked him why some get it and some don't. "Is it a matter of being smart enough?"

His reply came back quickly, full of loving correction. "Charles, what we call 'intelligence' has little to do with how powerful our minds are. If that were the case, few would have access to God and to his blessings. And that would be depressing and wrong."

*

Let me put it as simply as I can. I notice that every time I think about Jesus or Siddhartha or Kannon or Allah, I feel differently. I don't know what it is. The sensation is nearly impossible to describe. It's like suddenly walking into a forest of beech trees and seeing the light filtering down through the leaves. Or like being on the ocean when the fog lifts and the sky meets the water.

These moments—these *haiku* moments—connect me to what is truly real. I am sure Matsuo Bashō understood them too, as did Spencer W. Kimball and many others, be they men or women. From my experience, I know that anyone who does the will of God, anyone who makes an effort to rake, is blessed with such moments.

> fishing with Harriet
> in the fog of Monomoy—
> *mono no aware* (the sadness of all things)

As the years pass, my raking has made the veil of forgetfulness—the original thickness of the shell that surrounds my soul—a bit thinner. Will the truth get through the still remaining millimeters of that resilient something that prevents my nothingness? Surely, the words of the sacrament prayers "that they may always remember him" are an injunction to keep Jesus in mind as we go about our day-to-day. But maybe they're also asking us to remember an actual moment, the "time before time," when we were with him.

Who were we then, before we were born? What did we promise to do during our season here on earth?

In a former life, on that day when we decided to become mortal, what did we feel when we looked each other in the eye and said, "If it has to be done, then let's do it." What did we think we might accomplish here in this life?

The abiding "shape" of Zen's nothingness also becomes clearer to me. We are friends, you and I. Despite my shyness, my tendency to judge, my inadequacies, I share a purpose with you. It has taken me a long time to understand what "no poor among them" really means. Everyone is poor because there is no such thing as someone else and, therefore, no such problem as someone else's poverty.

> as I rake and rake—
> my new heart begins to feel
> a new poverty

Thankfully, my life has been mercifully extended. Without the love of many, without the grace of the gods, I would have died long before I discovered my deepest feelings of loyalty and happiness.

> across the blue sky—
> the cirrus clouds stretch
> from here to there

Barbara Richan

BUDDHISTS BELIEVE THAT OUR PRESENT LIFE IS ONE AMONG many, thus *re*-incarnation. Who we are now depends on who we were before. There is another round coming, the one we are preparing for now.

Future Bodhisattvas leave the burning house to learn justice, to push through sorrow, and to turn from their false conceptions of Truth. They turn away from the Buddha to embrace their own Buddha nature. They become compassionate enough to return to the burning house from which we all came—once upon a time, back then. We go back to that same broken place—to the torn walls, the scarred floors. We do so in order to help those still in delusion. This circular path is the Great Paradigm. For Buddhists, Christians, Jews, and Muslims it has this same shape, the path always curving so we see neither the future nor the past. Leaving, learning, sorrowing, rebelling, returning.

We turn once. To God. We turn twice. Away from God. Only by turning both *to* and *away* do we discover our godly nature.

In the end, we listen to the persistent voice that tells us, "What are you looking for, anyway? Just go home. You'll find it there."

I write about this path in *The End of the World, Plan B*. This is the first time I write so openly about such personal matters. I only do so because I feel that time is running out—not for the world, necessarily, but for "*my* world," for my own process of shedding the self and seeing this twofold idea of "the end of the world" for what it really is.

Is the end of the world a calamity? Or a purpose?

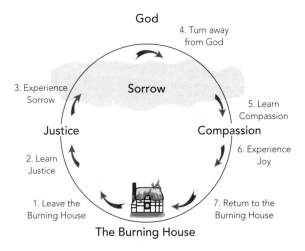

Figure 2. The Plan of Happiness

1. Leave the Burning House (walk away from delusion). 2. Learn justice (choose the right). 3. Experience sorrow (realize the sadness of justice—that is, punishment for all). 4. Turn away from God (learn disappointment and question your understanding of God). 5. Learn compassion (discover your own godliness). 6. Experience joy (realign with, and become one with God and your own godly nature). 7. Return to the Burning House (mediate, save others).

I am assigned another person to home teach. I know Barbara Richan only from a distance. She is older. She has perfect hair and a clean 2005 Toyota Camry.

> there on the back seat—
> an umbrella for the rain
> a hat for the sun

I begin visiting her. Each time I do, I wonder, "What in the world could we possibly have in common?"

Over time, I discover the obvious truth yet again. What we have in common is God's love, pure and simple. That's it. We share hope. We share nothingness, Allah's infinite mercy, Amida's compassion. We share sharing.

We do not share the *New York Times*, *umeboshi*, my over-and-under Browning shotgun, Bach's *Saint Matthew's Passion*, decaf lattes, National Public Radio, or Wittgenstein. But what we do share is more important than all those things. We share the common source of all things.

As Barbara's health begins to decline, her adult perfection gives way to a youthful, even childlike version of herself. Her dear friend Lori Parkinson moves in with her in order to see to her needs. What might have been a short stay becomes a long journey. Three years, in and out of the hospital.

I help in a peripheral way—putting up railings in the bathroom, shoveling the snow, mowing the lawn (with Kan's help).

At one low point along the way, Barbara ends up in the Lahey Hospital in Burlington. Kenny Bement and I visit. (I'm in another bishopric.) To us, she seems hopelessly ill. She struggles for breath. Her face is pallid.

We give her a blessing of release, which are words offered to those who are about to die. They are meant to be a gentle send-off and thanks. But Barbara revives, as if to shame us for giving up on her too soon.

*

I keep visiting Barbara. Every time I do, her cat is there on her bed. Such a loyal friend! My grandfather taught my father, and my father taught me. "Feed a dog for a day, and it will remember you for a hundred. Feed a cat for a hundred days, and it will remember you for one."

> such dedication!
> for over sixty-some years
> unfairness to cats

Barbara starts to fail again. While sitting at her bedside, I ask Lori if she's made any plans for a funeral.

"Why? Who would come?" she asks.

"You might be surprised."

In Zion, no one is forgotten.

It's not like I pull out my tape and start taking measurements for a coffin. But we do continue talking about "the end."

Turns out, Barbara is listening to every word. The next morning, she makes another remarkable comeback. She's not about to give up so easily.

*

As her body slowly weakens, Barbara starts speaking her own language. She addresses people Lori and I can't see. But when the Spirit is there with us, we connect with each other and have pleasant conversations in a language we all understand.

She smiles. She laughs.

I prepare a simple lesson. I tell her about my dog Satsuki.

*

Satsuki's story goes like this. "If Rei and I have one regret, it's that we didn't take Satsuki to puppy school. She's a sweet dog. But she never mastered the basic command to 'come.'"

Apparently, "come" is the hardest command for a dog to learn. Why? Because if our dogs don't come, we get upset. Who would go to a master who is angry?

I tell Barbara about our walks. We're going down the path. Satsuki smells something interesting and wanders off on her own. I call. No response.

I get frustrated.

"I say 'come' more loudly. Satsuki comes, but only *some* of the time."

Barbara suddenly perks up. She sits straight up and says, "*Then that's not 'come'!*"

Lori and I laugh. Barbara laughs too.

"Exactly right! Coming *some* of the time is really not 'come.' When God says, 'Come,' and you come some of the time, that's not 'come'!"

*

I continue the lesson.

"You know, hunting dogs are often trained with an electric collar. I once thought their purpose was to deliver a shock for bad behavior. But it's not quite like that."

My hunting partner, Ken Hafen, explained it to me this way. "I turn the collar on. But at as low a level as I can. When Hank starts misbehaving, I push the button that sends him a pulse. As soon as he changes his behavior, I take my finger off. Sooner or later, Hank learns he has the power to rid himself of that bad feeling."

It makes sense. The difference between pushing a button to deliver punishment and releasing a button to deliver reprieve is huge. When you think about it, repentance works the same way. The gods actually don't punish us the moment we do something wrong. They give us a little time to experience "that bad feeling."

And that bad feeling can be very subtle. So subtle, we can even ignore it, even to the point of becoming "past feeling." For this very reason, the ability to develop sensitivity is important. If we are actually going to rid ourselves of our burdens, it takes awareness. It takes an unflagging will to feel the most subtle types of "bad feelings" that people can have. None of that is possible if our sensitivity is clouded by "the self." Only in nothingness do we understand our feelings for what they are, *and* for what they can become.

Raking once in a while won't do it. As my mother would say, "The important thing is to make an effort." For life to be meaningful, we have to mean what we do. We can't just go through the motions of being good, righteous, understanding, and so on. We have to try to be constant in a world that is constantly distracting us, playing to our need to be entertained.

*

Every once in a while, one of my students will miss a class and ask me the next day, "Did I miss anything important?"

I always say, "No. Not really." But what I'm really thinking is, "Of course you missed something important! Why would we have class *one* time if class weren't important *every* time? Why don't you understand that?"

Life is short. There is no time to waste. Constant raking. No missing class.

Wash the dishes. Sweep the floor. Rake, rake, rake. To feel happiness, do a simple thing the right way. Do it now.

*

When I used to crawl under a truck to put grease in the fittings, my father would say, "Don't just go through the motions." Sometimes it was hard to get the grease to go in. You had to really want to make it happen for it to happen. Sometimes that meant crawling out from under the truck, moving the vehicle forward an inch or two, then crawling back under.

*

Barbara dies. We have a funeral. We don't fill the chapel. But a number of us meet in the Relief Society room.

I ask those present, "Why did Barbara hold on for so many years? Why did she have to suffer that long, final stretch?"

In the end, I think her suffering was a gift to the rest of us. It gave me and Lori and Michiko and everyone else a chance to live up to our ideals. While helping her, we forgot about ourselves.

> farewell, Barbara!—
> I will miss our visits and
> shoveling your snow

A Hard Thing

I AM IN THE BISHOP'S OFFICE IN THE BELMONT CHAPEL. ALONG with three others, we have been given the difficult assignment of holding a disciplinary council for two men in our ward who have recently married.

*

I'm sure it sounds false when we encourage them to continue participating in our ward. We say we love them. They are our brothers. But once they are out the door, we never see them in the pews again.

They feel unwanted. Who can blame them?

*

Our opening to the world allows us to accept the decrees of heaven. But didn't Jesus say we shouldn't be judgmental? When Abraham learns of the impending destruction of Sodom and Gomorrah, why does he question God's plan?

In the book of Jacob in the Book of Mormon, when the Lord of the vineyard decides to burn his unfruitful trees, his *servant* is the one who pleads with him to give them another chance. I don't think this means that the Lord doesn't know what he's doing. I think the force of this is, rather, that God is testing us. He's teaching us, his servants, how to mediate for others by posing a difficult question. Does punishment have to happen?

Surely, one purpose of the commandments is to help us feel a godly sorrow for how wayward our world is. But the sadness that flows from a well-developed sense of right and wrong is also meant to teach us *not* to judge others. The Atonement teaches us that our deeper purpose is to mediate for all those who fall short, not appeal to justice. Like Abraham, Noah, Moses, and Jesus, like Allah and Mohammed, like Kannon and Amida, you and I are also meant to take a place in the middle—pleading for all sinners (ourselves included) that they might be forgiven and restored.

The modern world came to misunderstand something fundamental. Justice was never meant to be the highest goal of society. Justice is like food. We can't do without it. But too much kills us. The purpose of justice is to get us beyond justice. Just as the purpose of reason is to get us beyond reason. What is the sound of one hand clapping?

*

Noah jumps down off the ark. His feet sink into the mud. He and his family have survived the end of the world.

At this point, does he shout, "We did it!"? No. In his great sorrow, in his anger, he makes God swear he will never send another flood.

> above the Wasatch—
> the colors of the rainbow
> bridge the open sky

When Kannon considered the sadness of the world, her head exploded. When it grew back, she had eleven heads—with more eyes to see more sorrow. In response, she also grew more arms with many more hands to help those in need.

It might well be beyond our ability to determine who is and is not sinful. Justice is blind in more ways than one. Yet it is *not* beyond our ability to have compassion for those who need our support.

> was it he or she?—
> I dreamed I met Kannon with
> her many heads and arms

All sentient beings have a divine potential. Mahayana Buddhists call it Buddha nature. Latter-day Saints call the process by which this divinity develops eternal progression. The purpose of life is to find, understand, and nurture this potential.

When we do, we come to truly feel the burden of life's sorrow. This is why Bodhisattvas and Saviors on Mount Zion don't eat and drink their fill of justice. Rather, they push through the sorrow that justice brings in order to gain compassion. They embrace the Atonement and plead for all, including bad cops, pharmaceutical executives who push OxyContin, and leaders who lie.

Without mercy, we are lost. The end of the world isn't about justice and the destruction of evil. It's about mercy and a fullness of revelation, which is what apocalypse actually means.

The end of the world is the Atonement, which started long ago. The end started at the very beginning.

My nephew Danny comes over for dinner. We are washing the dishes, and he says, "Uncle, I'm gay."

We discuss this and that. I don't love him any less.

> Paul used to be Saul—
> holding the robes of the
> stone throwers

As I grow older, the sharp categories of understanding that I learned as a child soften. The Taoist model of yin and yang proposes that in every male there is some female, and in every female there is some male. I come to believe that this lack of purity is an often unspoken truth about gender as it relates to our progression as loving people. Only at the central point of *wu ji*, the inexhaustible absence of extremes (無極), are we truly able to love (and to be) both male and female, bond and free, black and white, rich and poor.

This is a hard concept for many to understand. The modern ideas that structure our world continue to generate unhappiness and misunderstanding even for a restored "primitive church" that never was meant to be modern. In the April 2013 session of general conference, Boyd K. Packer, the late President of the Quorum of the Twelve, speaks about the dangers of being overly tolerant. In "These Things I Know," he makes the point that virtue can become vice when taken too far.

At the conclusion of this conference, President Thomas S. Monson stresses, "May we be tolerant of, as well as kind and loving to, those who do not share our beliefs and our standards. The Savior brought to this earth a message of love and goodwill to all men and women. May we ever follow His example."[1] For me, this comment and the way the prophet pauses after saying the word *tolerant* seem like a gentle response to Brother Packer's talk. It is possible to be overly *tolerant*. But this doesn't mean we should be intolerant.

*

Perhaps the prophet was sending a warning to those who might twist Brother Packer's words in unintended ways. Many of us, myself included, see ourselves as peacemakers even when the stability we seek is making life miserable for many. Racism, sexism, and other forms of modern judgment are oppressive in their attempt to establish "law and order." We fear disorder, but what purpose does harmony serve? "Suppose ye that I am come to give peace on earth? I tell you, Nay; but rather division" (Luke 12:51).

Jesus's peace is not the peace the world offers. His order is not a worldly order. "The weak things of the world shall come forth and break down the mighty and strong ones, that man should not counsel his fellow man, neither trust in the arm of flesh—But that every man might speak in the name of God the Lord, even the Savior of the world" (Doctrine and Covenants 1:19–20).

*

To be sure, President Packer and President Monson were both correct. Everything cannot be tolerated. Good is not bad. Bad is not good. Yet it is also true that we all experience life differently, even as we experience the same things. And it is also true that we start from different places, facing different kinds of challenges. This being the case, we need to be tolerant and kind. Being moral and strictly obedient to God's laws should fill us with "love and goodwill." Fascists seek purity, but they do not have pure hearts..

Surely, this is one reason why the Atonement is a gift to *all.* Toward the same end, the two great commandments—to love God and to love others—teach us to be generous.

Justice is not our goal. Jesus made this perfectly clear. Having clarified who "the blessed" are—the mournful, the meek, the poor in heart, those who desire righteousness, the pure hearted, the peacemakers—he went on to teach that, in the end, the rain falls on *everybody.* "For he maketh his sun to rise on the evil and on the good, and sendeth rain on the just and unjust" (Matthew 5:45). Why be obedient if blessings come to the disobedient? Jesus's answer is clear. Everyone deserves to be blessed because no one deserves to be blessed. That is the meaning of his condescension, kenosis, and sacrifice. This is love's senseless loyalty.

> in the tree's deep shade—
> sunlight spreads over the plains
> of nothingness

> natural history—
> the dinosaurs all turned gay
> and went extinct

When I ask others about this moment when Brother Packer and President Monson together taught us about the two sides of tolerance, very few remember it. Most missed it entirely.

Note

1. Thomas S. Monson, "Until We Meet Again," churchofjesuschrist.org /study/general-conference/2013/04/until-we-meet-again (2:07).

CHAPTER 24

A Father's Concerns,
Joan Again

Leif graduates from Tufts with flying colors. He gets a job with a new-age company where most of the employees are younger than thirty and you can eat cornflakes and gummy bears in the office.

He prospers. But the struggle that every twenty-something must face—to know who you truly are—bears down on him.

He comes home for a respite. Being around family and eating familiar food is strengthening.

I offer to give him a blessing, and he readily accepts. For the first time, I get angry while holding my hands on someone's head. To the spirits who threaten my boy's peace, I yell, "Get away from my son. You can't have him!"

Yes, many of our troubles are chemical reactions, not attacks by dark angels. But who created the chemical world? And how much influence do we have over it?

Mie's marriage doesn't last. We all love her husband, especially Kan. When Kan asks me why we don't see Ryan as much as before, I find it hard to explain. "Mie and Ryan love each other 9, but to be married you need to be 10."

I feel Mie's suffering, and wish I could do more to help. She goes off to Berlin for the summer to learn German and to make a decision.

> in the warm spring sun—
> the willows glow yellow green
> the maples crimson

I keep raking. One spring evening, Joan Sheahan calls the Arlington police. They arrive. She tells them about the people living in the walls of her house. They put her in an ambulance and send her to the Faulkner Hospital.

Over the next few weeks, tests are done. Interviews are held. A lawyer shows up. Her sons are given legal control over her affairs. They find accommodations for her in an "old folks' home" in Lexington.

Joan shares a room with an unfriendly woman who is bound to her wheelchair. The place feels like a jail and smells like a urinal.

A fill-in-the-blank poster in the hallway reads

> Today is: <u>Sunday</u>.
> The season is: <u>winter</u>.
> The date is: <u>January 17, 2016</u>.
> The weather is: <u>clear and cool</u>.
> The next holiday is: <u>Valentine's Day</u>.

Surrounded by stands of towering white pines, the red brick nursing home seems decent enough from the outside. But the residents are an odd mix of elderly people and young men recently released from prison. One day, a revolt breaks out, and the two factions join forces. Young and old start throwing furniture from the second-floor balcony onto the lobby floor below.

Joan finally gets permission to leave. She moves in with her son Robbie for a few months.

The Sheahan boys spring into action. They start cleaning up the Arlington house with a plan to sell it. After a few weeks, though, they tire of filling dumpster after dumpster with the things their mother has collected over the years. Clothes that no longer fit, shoes of every possible style and color, fireplace gratings, flashlights, old-fashioned irons made of cast iron, bottles of water and juice, cans of food well past their expiration date. They decide to sell the place as is, even though it means a reduced sales price.

They move Joan to a long-term facility in Burlington, not far from the mall. It's a much nicer place. Joan has her own bedroom and a small sitting room with a sink and mini refrigerator.

She's the youngest woman there. For that reason alone, Joan jokes about being "a hot item." I think she's making it up. But then I visit her a few weeks later and she introduces me to her new boyfriend.

His name is Anthony. He used to be a factory electrician. He plays the piano. "Ya here to check me out?" He extends a hand in friendship. He's charming.

"Any friend of Joan's is a friend of mine."

I'm happy for her. I knew her former boyfriend. He was a slightly morose electrical engineer who was always trying to help Joan get her affairs in order. He finally faded from the scene when she rejected his advice to sell the house and move back to Canada. (In this way, he and I saw Joan's situation similarly.)

Although Burlington lies outside our ward boundaries, I keep visiting Joan. I know that when I reach the pearly gates and stand before my Maker, one question that will be in my mind is, "Did you learn to love Joan, or were you just going through the motions?"

CHAPTER 25

Nothingness, Haiku, and the *Shimenawa*

I am driving down Massachusetts Avenue, returning home after teaching early morning seminary. I teach with Mike and Rebecca Zimmer, who have recently moved to Arlington from the Washington, DC, area. Our pupils are high school students who get up every morning at 5:30 a.m. to study the scriptures. Last year, we focused on the New Testament. This year, it's the Book of Mormon.

Despite all the bad news coming from Washington, DC, I'm feeling hopeful. As I wait for the light to turn green, I think about my volleyball friends in Kyoto, who are now running their own temples. I also think about that fateful day in Palo Alto, when I was told that if I kept my focus on loving people, things would eventually work out. To a surprising degree, things actually are turning out pretty well. Slowly, step by step, my weakness is turning into a strength.

At Tufts, I am team teaching a new class with Stephen White, professor of philosophy. His wide reading has helped make him the warm and open-minded person he is. Our subject is "Nothingness." With a title like that, it's a wonder anyone signs up. But the seats fill up quickly.

On the first day of class, I ask our students, "Tell me. What do you think you're going to learn in this class anyway?" It's an honest question. I really want to know the answer.

Professor White teaches Hume, Kant, Romanticism, and the sublime. I teach animism, the *Heart Sutra*, Nagarjuna, Zen, and Nishitani (when we get that far). Stephen and I have a number of common interests—the reality of the self, philosophy of mind, artificial intelligence, and so on. But, because of my beginnings in south-central Utah as a Buddhist/Latter-day Saint, my intellectual path is unusual, even eccentric.

*

My life has been full of surprises. Perhaps the biggest surprise is the way my spiritual quest has found peace with my intellectual training. The two have become mutually supportive in a way I never would have predicted—and all because I was able to keep the focus on the two simple tasks of loving and being loved, even during many difficult years of wandering.

I can see that my decades-long study of Japanese literature, along with my long trek as a Latter-day Saint, has prepared me well for many of the intellectual trends that have unfolded during my career in academia. As someone who never did have a comfortable place in the mainstream of Western thought and civilization to begin with, and as someone who has always been cautious about the secular forces of modernity, I now have a head start in understanding things like

- life after modern hegemony,
- the resurgence of spiritual life,
- the new materiality,
- neoanimism,
- a return to locality and lyricism,
- the posthuman, and
- the end of the secular era.

The end of modernity means that not since the sixteenth century has the world seen so much cultural upheaval. Once banned by rationality and positivism, today monsters (*bakemono*) are making a comeback. Within the academy, we are witnessing a transitional period of great consequence. But what do we call this postmodern *something else* that now unfolds before us? Some call it the end of the world. But I see it as an age of renewal.

Ours is a replay of the Azuchi-Momoyama period, the bloody yet brilliant age of Hasegawa Tōhaku and Kanō Eitoku. It now returns as the troubled era of Higashiyama Kaii and Kusama Yayoi. Even the crude and blindly ambitious Oda Nobunaga has come back in the form of Trump, Putin, Duterte, Bolsonaro, and other authoritarian leaders. Ours is an age of heroes, of myth, of idolatry.

Although the fabric of society is being shredded as I speak, as a self-declared *sunshine* postmodernist, I perceive the possible blessings of this raging storm. If this is, indeed, the end of (modern) Truth, then I prefer to think of this time after modernity as an age of *many truths* rather than of *no Truth*. As the weaknesses of capitalism make themselves painfully obvious to us, we actually do know where to look for a way to establish Zion, a place where there are no poor among us.

I am browsing through a book on Zen ink painting at the Japanese School library in Medford. To my surprise, I learn that the painting above the fireplace in our living room—a boy riding an ox—is actually a Zen-inspired image with a very specific meaning. It is a picture of one of the ten steps of enlightenment.

I inherited this painting from my grandfather. Apparently, he was attracted to the image at first sight, and my uncle Henry bought it for him. That must have happened after the family left Wyoming and moved to Utah, adding to a few small things that have survived from the years before the Relocation—a small statue of Ninomiya Kinjirō, my father's athletic medals, and a pennant from the Rose Bowl.

For years, I thought the painting was of a peasant boy returning home after work, happy to have finished another hard day of labor. But then I suddenly discover it's not that at all. It's a depiction of that very moment when the ox (the sought-after truth) and the boy (the seeker of truth) are understood as identical.

Ox and boy. The seeker (boy) and sought-for Truth (ox) are one and the same.

> seeing differently—
> the farm boy and the truth
> are one and the same

This conflation of seeker and sought-after makes sense to me. How could we possibly know, or not know, who the gods are apart from understanding who we are? Isn't that the force of Moroni's promise—that we will see God as he is because we will become like him (see Moroni 7:48)?

Many of my students tell me they no longer believe in the traditions of their parents. They are "cultural Jews," "recovering Catholics," "inactive Mormons," "resistant Muslims," "incredulous Hindus," and "disinterested Protestants." At the same time, they are quick to tell me they're not insensitive to spiritual matters.

I wonder what this means. Perhaps my young friends are not rejecting spiritual reality so much as they dislike its symbolic packaging, and the all-too-human personalities of its heroes—Joseph Smith, who kept secrets from his dear Emma; Brigham Young, who embraced racism with his all-too-modern heart; Joseph Fielding Smith, who considered white people superior to all others. In these postmodern times, would it be possible to find a more direct, nonsymbolic, and less elitist and patriarchal access to this spiritual realm that is so hard to dismiss altogether?

To cultivate my students' ability to feel the power of the world directly, I teach them how to write haiku. (You've noticed by now that I've included many of these short poems in this book. I do so for the reasons I belatedly explain here.) Our sensei is Matsuo Bashō, the early-modern pseudo-priest who theorized premodern aesthetics at that juncture when "old ways" were being erased from memory by the dawning of modern thought.

Some of Bashō's principles of poetic creation are these:

- *Kōgo kizoku* ("Rise high and return to the low")
- *Butsuga ichi'nyo* ("Become one with all things")
- *Fueki ryūkō* ("Embrace the unchanging and the ever-changing")

Haiku are born of lyrical experience. To help my students understand their emotional relationship with the world, I have them come up with poems that are simple and direct and oriented toward the thingness of nouns, shunning the descriptive and interpretive force of adjectives and adverbs. Haiku are neither word candy nor conceptual intrigue. They are simpler, humbler. They express an awareness of poetic reality, experience at its most basic concrete level, at the level of what I have been calling raking.

A good haiku allows you to see the moment of its creation. A great one allows you to see *and feel* that instant. Its power comes from perceiving the attraction of things (*mono*) as directly as possible.

This direct tie to materiality is why some of Bashō's greatest haiku are little more than simple declarations. When the poet visited Matsushima, he was so overwhelmed by the beauty of the pine-covered isles that he was unable to write anything at all. Later, when he was finally able to come up with a verse, he wrote this puzzling poem.

> Matsushima
> Ah, Matsushima
> Matsushima
>
> Matsushima ya
> Aah, Matsushima ya
> Matsushima ya
>
> 松島や
> ああ松島や
> 松島や

Why is this even a poem? It's a question worth asking.

*

Haiku capture a lyrical moment. They express the below-the-line realm of material, visible things. These short poems are an engagement with thingness itself, expressions of the power that we feel from concrete reality.

That power is also recognized by the cultural practice of tying a *shimenawa*, a straw rope, around trees, rocks, and other sacred things and places. Like a haiku, the rope similarly points to that which is visible, near, and approachable. It tells us that the gods are not far away. In their tenderness and anger, they animate all that is near, and dear, to us.

The *shimenawa* could be one answer to the postmodern dilemma of how we come together in a world of diversity. It might help us make sense of the sacred again by making possible a nonsymbolic approach to the material reality on which we depend. If it

A *shimenawa*, nonsymbolic sign of the sacred.

is the symbolic packaging of religion that my students reject, then here is a ribbon that is not an unwanted wrapping.

Once again, the rope draws attention to that which is impressive and *present*. It expresses neither itself, nor something other than what it surrounds. It says, simply, "The sacred is here, in front of you."

Tree, rock, waterfall, fish, people. God not only made them, but he gave each a measure of his spirit. All things are spiritual. "For I, the Lord God, created all things, of which I have spoken, spiritually, before they were naturally upon the face of the earth" (Moses 3:5).

I travel to Matsue. I visit the Izumo Shrine, the second most holy site in Japan. I speak with one of the priests.

I tell him that I'm from Boston. "We have a huge beech tree on our campus," I explain. "I was wondering if it would be all right to put a *shimenawa* around it?"

I ask because I'm not sure such a thing has ever been done in the New World before. I expect criticism. But, without hesitating, the priest says, "If you think the tree has some sort of power, go ahead. Do it."

Few conversations have ever made me happier. I believe it was Kamo no Chōmei who said that "a beautiful place has no owner."

> a *shimenawa*—
> the empty cicada shell (*utsusemi* 空蝉)
> flies ever skyward

The priest affirms what I have studied about animism. In its original form, it has neither organization nor doctrine. It is essentially a local (*jimoto* 地元) phenomenon. It is about the feelings we have for our immediate surroundings. Not being a symbol of anything, the *shimenawa* simply marks sacred places for our attention.

Faith, then, develops and matures not as theological speculation but as practical involvement.

The nonsymbolic *shimenawa* reminds me of something we all do differently that is the same: we take things (*mono*) from the world in order to live. Is this our point of commonality—this and none other? If we focus here, might we become a society that cares about the earth and its welfare? A Zion of one heart and mind, where there are no poor?

I return to Boston. After discussing my thoughts about *shimenawa* with the Tufts administration and chaplaincy, I plan a ceremony. I invite my colleagues and students to help me put a rope around the giant beech tree that graces the slope just south of Ballou Hall.

Vicky Cirrone, our department administrator, helps me throw a party. About sixty people attend. We have food. One of my students supplies the band. His father is there to help.

*

My hopes are high. But a few weeks later, on commencement night, three undergraduates cut down the rope. They describe themselves as "nihilists." I would like to meet them, but they quickly leave town so we can't discuss their motivations. To this day, they have not named themselves to me.

A small group of my students, Joe Wat and a few others, help me repair the rope. We put it back up. We have our own small, second celebration. There is a guitar and singing. We sit on the grass, facing the tree, in a semicircle.

> kumbaya croissant—
> cross-legged around the rope
> around the beech tree

By August, the *shimenawa* disappears.

A *shimenawa* at Tufts University.

I don't know who takes it down, or why. My guess is that someone thinks it symbolizes something they don't like or under-stand—a religion, an organization, a movement, or a particular set of ideological values. Or maybe they just like their beech trees plain, which would make the most sense to me.

But, here again, my critics are not brave enough to make themselves openly known to me or to anyone else. They are cowards.

The next year, I put up another rope. I have a sign built that says, "A *shimenawa* is a rope with tassels, tied around something sacred. It is not a symbol. It does not stand for anything. It does not point to a particular notion or conception. It simply marks something present, visible, approachable, and worthy of respect."

By August, the rope disappears again.

Not only that, but the giant tree gets struck by lightning and begins to die. The difficult decision to cut it down is made.

The administration asks me to lead a brief service to recognize the tree for the role it has played as a member of the Tufts community. It is seven stories tall and almost two hundred years old. President Tony Monaco is there at the funeral, as well as his predecessor, Larry Bacow, and Adele Bacow.

I move the *shimenawa* to an old cherry tree on higher ground, just in front of Bendetson Hall. This time the rope stays up. A year later, I replace it with another one made of rice straw that I purchase in Komagome, Tokyo, after a visit to Donald Keene and Uehara Seiki's apartment nearby.

This fourth rope eventually ends up on the ground. I'm not sure if someone cut it down or if the rain and the wind simply snapped its worn strands.

Either way, I'm resigned to dealing with the difficulties as they come. A renewed appreciation of the earth is not going to happen overnight. Surely, the Renewal will take many forms. We are not free from the selfishness and strife that has always marked any human attempt to understand power. One thing is clear, though. If we're going to remedy the environmental challenges that face us today, we will need to employ all the scientific *and* spiritual knowledge we can muster. Practical problems are spiritual problems. Spiritual problems are practical.

We need to learn how to share both the good and bad of what we love and of what we hate.

> beneath the beech tree—
> physicists and poets
> all picnic on fractals
>
> I sit down to eat
> the entire universe
> but forget the salt

CHAPTER 26

The Family I Wanted

Rei works hard. I often worry that she's not getting enough sleep.

She's trying to keep up with her teaching and also with directing the Japanese Program at Northeastern University. She's also in the middle of creating an online workbook for her students. The workload is overwhelming.

We share the cooking and cleaning and Kan's training. It's hard, but we can handle it. Still, Rei's visiting teachers—Amy Duke and Anna Dunnavin—insist on bringing us dinner one night. A green salad, a loaf of bread from the Wilson farm, lasagna, and gingerbread for dessert.

I am touched that these two women care about us enough to do this. The spirit of the sisters of Sigurd, Utah, is alive and well in the Yale- and Harvard-educated sisters of the Arlington Ward. Despite their different paths, all these women share the same simple faith. They dedicate themselves to their neighbors' welfare.

gratitude—
the calling geese skim above
the oak forest

Being married to Rei is a great blessing. I am glad I listened to my sister Charlotte's advice. Both my sisters, Charlotte and Annie, have been looking out for me. Mie and Rei join the fray.

Now that I know the difference between a good and bad marriage, I try to have family home evening every week and family prayer every day. Being able to do so is a great blessing—the greatest of blessings, in fact.

Mie seems happier these days. She writes a dissertation proposal and gets a committee together. Her work as a graduate student is stressful, but she's learning a lot and enjoying her studies.

The Inouye family, Lexington, 2013. From left: Mie, Charles, Satsuki, Kan, Rei, Leif.

New Haven isn't that far away. We make a point of getting together with Mie and Leif once a month. Being a family is one thing. Behaving like a family is another.

> stir fry and steamed rice—
> Mie smiles at a message
> on her cell phone

Leif gets a promotion and moves into a new house. He's learning how to bake bread. Maybe, someday, he'll learn how to make sugar cookies. He buys ten New Hampshire chickens and builds a coop.

He gets a dog and names her Kumo, which means "cloud" 雲.

> Thanksgiving morning
> I meet my first granddaughter—
> half beagle, half pit bull

Kumo has an interesting past, one that we piece together by conjecture. She apparently lived six years or so in an Atlanta shelter, then came north to avoid the hurricanes of last summer. Indoors, she's slow-moving and sweet. Outdoors, she's a free spirit, a sprinter and intrepid hunter.

*

One morning, Kumo runs out the door and into the woods. When I find her, she's looking up into a tree.

> high in the branches
> sneering down at dog and man—
> a raccoon god

Observing the treed animal, I remember the morning when Wilson Rawls visited Gunnison Valley High School many years ago. Rawls wrote *Where the Red Fern Grows*, a novel Mr. Vest read to our sixth-grade class.

During the Q and A that followed his talk, I raised my hand and asked, "Mr. Rawls, did you really chop down that big tree?"

"Well, I cut down *a* tree," he responds.

Our Toyota Camry is thirteen. Rei and I have been married for thirteen years. Satsuki is thirteen.

Like other Labrador retrievers, Satsu has always been very food oriented. When she suddenly stops eating the one brand of dog food she has always loved, we're alarmed. We're afraid she's getting ready to leave us.

She has good days and bad. One morning she's a little more energetic than usual. We go for a short walk in the Sutherland Woods behind our house on Peacock Farm Road. Once able to catch a ball while running full speed, she now hobbles along.

> Satsuki and I
> move one slow step at a time—
> crimson maple leaves

It's been a warm autumn, but the time comes to start a fire in the fireplace. The trees outside flare a thousand hues of green and yellow and red. I still love the gray, cold skies of November.

> the wind I once feared
> is now a source of comfort—
> Zion and Zen

Kan, now seven years old, is a good helper. We rake leaves together in the yard.

> pressed down,
> shaken and running over—
> fifteen bags of leaves

I am thankful for my family and for my home.

> this is life eternal—
> hauling firewood and
> washing dishes

CHAPTER 27

Another Hard Week

TUESDAY MORNING IN MID-DECEMBER.

Satsuki walks around the house once. Comes in the back door. Barks and collapses.

We lay her down on her bed. We watch as her heart slows and stops.

"Go ahead, Satsu. Don't be afraid."

I pat her head and close her eyes.

After thirteen years and seven months, she's gone.

Rei cries out in grief. "She told us she was going."

We taught Satsuki to be communicative, and she was to the very end.

＊

Kan is in school. He gets off the bus. He and Rei walk up the slope to the house. Once inside, he takes off his coat and snow pants.

Rei asks him. "Do you notice anything different?"

He doesn't.

"Satsuki died this morning."

Kan wails. The tears flow.

For the first few years of Kan's life, he and Satsuki were rivals. But they eventually became good friends.

*

The next morning, Kan asks me, "Is Satsuki going to come back?"

"No, she's not," I answer. "But maybe we'll see her again someday." I don't really have an answer.

*

Nothing brings me out of my shell, out of my isolation and weakness, more than having a wife, two sons, a daughter, and a dog. Family life is raking at its best and most difficult. In families, we cannot avoid difficult people and situations. We *are* those difficult people. We are those difficult situations. Given this opportunity to not escape from our weaknesses, we learn how to be kind and thoughtful by caring for each other. We find solutions to the problems that come along.

On Wednesday, I dig a grave in the backyard. I choose a spot near a black pine I've recently planted. It's not an easy dig. The ground is frozen. I hit many rocks and have to chop through many roots from a nearby oak tree.

But this is a good place. Satsuki will be just outside Kan's window. He'll be able to look out and see where she's lying.

*

I once asked my father why I liked dogs so much.

He replied as if the answer were totally obvious. "Because you're lonely."

It's true. All my life I have loved dogs. And all my life I *have* been lonely. But I am no longer in denial about my need for people, even for the ones who make me uncomfortable. Despite my shyness and my reflex to retreat, I now know that I need the world, that I sincerely care about it. Knowing this brings enough happiness to counter any disappointment.

Satsuki was not a person, of course. But my connection to her is just as deep and abiding. I wake up in the middle of the night. My heart hurts. I am literally suffering from heartache.

The Four Noble Truths require that I rid myself of attachments. In my mind, I can accept the truth of all things changing. But my heart lags behind.

To rephrase my father's statement about reading, "People who don't love, live once. But people who love, live many times." The problem with living many times is that we also die many times—all in one short lifetime.

✻

I build a coffin. It's three feet long by two feet wide. Rei and I line it with a brightly colored beach towel. I run to Trader Joe's to buy flowers. I get a white bouquet for Satsuki. For Rei, I get one like it, with a few red roses mixed in.

I've been touched by the care that Rei extended to Satsuki during her final days. Rei fed her by hand, one piece of softened dog food at a time. I wasn't capable of doing as much.

✻

We place Satsuki in her pine box. We put one of Rei's sweaters over her and add a layer of linen. We set her outside for the night. The temperatures will dip to about 15 degrees. To keep her away from the coyotes, we put her on a platform made of saw horses and two-by-fours. We leave the yard lights on.

> how bitterly cold!—
> all that warms the universe
> is the porch light

> howling at the moon—
> the hungry coyotes move
> through the snowy woods

I get up early. Satsuki has made it through the night safely.

I go teach seminary and come back.

At 7:15 a.m., Eric Kramer, my neighbor across the street, comes over to help me lift a boulder out of the hole I'm digging for Satsu's grave. I tried to get it out by myself, but it's just too big for one person.

I ask Eric if he'd like to say goodbye. He pays his respects.

> *bang, bang, bang, bang, bang—*
> Eric drives a nail into
> the yellow pine boards

We keep Kan home from school in the morning. He makes a card. We put it in the coffin.

To Satsuki from our family

Dear Satsuki,
I'm sorry you died. But you had to die. See you again.
Kan

We put the bouquet of white flowers in with Satsu. We nail the last two boards in place. We carry her to the backyard and lower her into the ground.

We say a prayer.

The mound of soil is frozen. We use a pick to break through to the softer dirt. A shovelful at a time, Satsuki's yellow coffin disappears beneath its final covering of earth. I roll the boulder Eric and I lifted out of the hole into place. It will make a nice headstone.

> rest well, Satsuki—
> three blue jays feed noisily
> in the fresh snow

This wintry weather makes me think of my grandfather. We used to take a bucket of hot water to pour over the frozen pig trough on days like this. How many years has it been since we made our way across that snowy yard together?

My parents also died as winter approached. Now when I go back to Utah, my mother's flower garden is gone. My memories of my father are still so painful that I cannot bear to go out to see the farm.

CHAPTER 28

Visit from an Old Friend

ONE DAY, WHILE VISITING MY FAMILY IN UTAH, I FINALLY force myself to go out to the Arnold farm. I walk into one of the potato pits. On the concrete floor, the eroding clay walls have become spreading fans of silt.

> talk to me, Daddy—
> the tractors you once drove
> are quietly rusting
>
> the family farm—
> through a squirrel hole
> comes a ray of hope

Everyone tried hard. My grandparents, my parents, my uncles and aunts, my sister Charlotte, Henry Timican, Alice John, Joe the Navajo worker, my brother Dillon, Warren's wife Susan, my cousin Tats, Daniel Von Dwornick, Kerry Duke, Marc Butler, the swimmer at Crane's Beach, Matt Burnett, David Johnston, Barbara Richan. I myself have nearly died a few times. With each experience of death, the sustaining power of life becomes more understandable to me.

Someday, when I experience the end of the world, will there be brightness and clarity? Will I be with my family and friends? Or will I be alone, still trapped within my prison of self-concern?

One thing I am glad to have learned is that death is not the end of us. I know this with certainty and grow a little happier each day. The disappointments and setbacks still come. But I now know that they are temporary and that someday I will be with those who have gone before me.

Beyond this life is an eternal sociality, a reflection of what we are experiencing here on earth. In the next life, there will be families and friendships, connections and affiliations, concern and caring, sin and repentance, forgetting and learning. Knowing this continuity is comforting to me. In the celestial kingdom, the Pure Land, the Western Paradise—there will be another garden to rake someday.

As comforting as the future is, it doesn't really make sense to look forward to the next life, or to want to die. Yesterday and tomorrow will always be less important than today. And today will always be less important than the moment we call *now*. The concrete now is more important than the theoretical now, although we cannot know one without the other.

There are things to do now. We live below the line, in the physical moment, with bodies that weigh something, with a mind that knows something. The link between one hopeful instance and another is a dream and a prayer. It is a poem, a flash and fading of the nothingness that is the sum of what we share, the beauty that has no owner.

> tidings of great joy—
> the winter wind moves quickly
> through the frozen woods

Charles in his Zen meditation garden. Lexington, 2020.

a flickering fire—
newspaper and kindling
moistened with tears

If we keep raking, our weaknesses can be changed into strengths. Someday I hope to escape the pull of the great and spacious building altogether, to stand up to the sullen invaders who descend in helicopters and planes. All-knowing, grim, sure of the Truth, my enemies try to hold me back. But, in the end, I'll be freed from the hallways and offices that have kept me prisoner to status and ambition. I'll be free of judgment. I'll be filled with compassion.

across the dark sky—
the stars of the Silver Pavilion
raked into rows

Leaving myself behind, I rush toward the burning house, rake in hand.

where's Uncle Bob?—
My shattered crystal ball is
glued together again

I knock on the door. It opens.

No-self. I am marrow in the bone and strength in the sinews. The gods are not distant. Neither are they invisible nor hard to know. They are all around us.

In every soul, in each heart, there is boundless poverty. But to know this poorness is to gain freedom from our delusions, including the common misunderstanding of death as the end of existence. Because of the Atonement, we are free to not be free. Gladly, willingly, we return to the burning house, to the endless suffering that is love.

We make friends. We marry. We have families. We form communities.

Sometimes, we squander our friendships. We get divorced. We lose loved ones. We remove ourselves from the very groups that would sustain us.

And yet, I cannot judge you. My own foolishness is without measure, my pride is unfathomable.

When the wind blows, I hear a sound. I see the moving trees. And though I can't tell from whence it comes or to where it lists, I know that the wind is real, and true, and full of life.

That moaning is now an old friend. Its ancient voice is a source of joy. As I lie next to Rei in our warm bed, I hear a breeze move up the hill. It roars through the frozen woods. It stirs the cherry, red oak, and white pine. I feel it. As it fades from my ears, I adjust my pillow and dream of hearing it again.

Glossary

Akutagawa Ryūnosuke (1892–1927)

A brilliant writer of short fiction who eventually lost his faith in language and literature and succumbed to his sense of unease. He is the author of "In the Grove," which is the basis of Kurosawa Akira's heralded film *Rashōmon.* There might be something we call truth, facts, reality, how things really are. But it is also true that ten people will see this same reality in ten different ways depending on their position relative to what they are trying to observe, relate to, depict, and so on.

Amida

A Bodhisattva noted for his mercy. He is the main focus of worship in Pure Land Buddhism, which began as a popularized form of the more esoteric, magic-oriented schools that were patronized by Japan's elite. For the masses, things were radically simplified. Just saying *"Namu Amida Butsu"* ("Praise to Amida") one time is enough to ensure one's salvation.

anatman (Sanskrit)

The Buddhist notion that there is no such thing as the self. On the most obvious level, self-concern, selfishness, self-aggrandizement, and self-pity are understandable as undesirable traits. But *anatman* is a denial of the intrinsic existence of the self. We cannot think of a self without having a notion of no-self. Nothing stands alone without being influenced by many other things. By knowing this interconnection between all things, we become more thoughtful and compassionate.

Atsumori

A Taira (or Heike) warrior who was killed during the battle of Ichi no Tani (1184) by Minamoto no Naozane. Upon engaging with an enemy warrior, Naozane could see that Atsumori was a beautiful young man, about the age of his own son. Although Naozane was loath to kill him, he had no choice since his position as a Minamoto warrior required that he honor form. After the battles against the Heike were over, Naozane renounced the world and became a Buddhist priest. In the Noh play named after the eponymous Atsumori, the two enemies meet again—one now a priest and the other a spirit from the dead. They clash again, but this time they find resolution and peace in the Buddhist law of compassion.

Azuchi-Momoyama

A period, used primarily by art historians, to indicate the years from 1568 to 1600, when Oda Nobunaga, from his castle at Azuchi, and Toyotomi Hideyoshi, from his castle in Momoyama, ruled Japan. This time of a great cultural flourishing coincided with the latter stages of a long period of consolidation that ended with the unification of the country under the hegemonic leadership of Oda Nobunaga, Toyotomi Hideyoshi, and Tokugawa Ieyasu. Characteristic developments of this period include colorful folding screens (*byōbu*), intense patronage of the tea ceremony, and the influence of Europeans who made their way to Japan for the first time.

Butsuga ichi'nyo 物我一如

"Become one with all things." Bashō taught that identification with the world must occur if one is to write poetry about it. What gets in our way of this empathetic understanding of reality is the self, which establishes a distance between us and everything else. What is required, then, is to rid ourselves of the self. This selflessness manifests itself as a lack of description and other forms of interpretation. You let the world be itself.

daikon

A long white radish. A common ingredient in Japanese cuisine.

dharma

The universal truth as taught by Buddhism and other south Asian spiritual traditions. Visually, the dharma is represented by a wheel that is constantly turning, thus holding the world together and making reality possible. Mahayana thinkers believed that the dharma was in a state of decline, and they called these latter days *mappō*, or "the end of the law." In this period of decline, a person cannot attain salvation on his or her own merits. Only the help of a savior, such as Amida or Kannon, makes salvation possible.

fueki ryūkō 不易流行

"The unchanging and the ever-changing." Bashō taught that in an evanescent world where everything is always changing, there still exists the consistency of form, perceived as principles, truths, patterns, and so on. To be able to write haiku, a grasp of both the changing and the unchanging is necessary. After all, how could seasonal change, a common theme of haiku, even be perceived without some conception of stasis? Only a sense of permanence allows us to notice change. That said, it is essentially important to realize that permanence is illusory. We often think of God as never-changing, but latter-day revelation shows us that he is always changing—weeping in response to our suffering, growing in light and truth. The same can be said of a person or a tree—seemingly they have a sense of permanence, yet they are always changing. Teenagers often suffer because they are learning about their permanence even as their bodies are changing and as society's demands on them rapidly evolve.

hakujin 白人

Literally, "white person." The term was commonly used by Japanese immigrants to the United States but is now avoided because of its stereotypical connotations—uncivilized, brash, and so on. Over time, people are realizing the harmful evil of racist stereotypes.

hana

Literally, "flower." As a generic term, it was anciently understood to mean plum blossoms. But at a certain point, sometime during the Heian period (794–1185), *hana* came to mean cherry blossoms, as in the following poem by the Zen priest Dōgen (1200–1253).

Haru wa hana,	In spring the cherry blossoms,
Natsu hototogisu,	In summer the cuckoo,
Aki wa tsuki,	In autumn the moon,
Fuyu yuki saete	And in wintertime the
Suzushikarikeri.	clear cold snow.

Hasegawa Tōhaku (1539–1610)

A painter of the Azuchi-Momoyama period, noted for his folding screens (*byōbu*). His painting of pine trees, done in different shades of sumi ink, is one of my favorite images in all of art.

Heart Sutra

The *Prajnaparamita Sutra* (*Heart of the Perfection of Wisdom*). As the most well-known and oft-quoted sutra among Mahayana practitioners, the *Heart Sutra* is notable for its rigorous denial of anything that claims permanent intrinsic existence. "There are no eyes, ears, nose, tongue, body, or mind; there are no forms, sounds, smells, tastes, feelings, or objects of mind." What is the point of this insistent negation? It is the spiritual understanding that nothing is unconditional, that all things are mutually dependent. An understanding of this concept is necessary for the nurturing of a compassionate and appreciative regard for all things.

Higashiyama Kaii (1908–1999)

A painter of Nihonga (Japanese painting) who became the most famous artist in post-War Japan. His works tended to be graphically simple, often images of forests and mountains. He was also a prolific writer, often writing on the theme of evanescence, in which he emphasized the importance of passivity. "I do not live. I've been made to live."

Hotei

The Laughing Buddha. Hotei is a semi-historical Chinese figure (Budai) who practiced Chan (Zen) Buddhism and claimed at the time of his death to be Maitreya, Buddha of the Future. In Japan, he is one of the Seven Gods of Fortune. Rotund, wearing loose clothing, and carrying a large sack filled with gifts, Hotei signals contentment and prosperity. He is beloved for his generosity and his ability to bring good fortune to those who place his image in their homes.

Issei 一世

First-generation immigrants from Japan to the United States. Most came to accumulate wealth and return to Japan, but some, like my grandparents, remained overseas. Brought to Hawaii to work as an indentured worker for three years, my grandfather Inouye fled from his plantation to the far side of the big island of Hawaii, where he met my grandmother and eventually moved to California.

Izumi Kyōka (1873–1939)

An eccentric writer who pursued a gothic vision of reality at a time when realism was becoming dominant. Ridiculed by many, Kyōka's admirers include many of the most famous authors of subsequent generations: Akutagawa, Tanizaki, Kawabata, Tsushima Yūko, and others. Criticized by his contemporaries for his old-fashioned belief in monsters, ghosts, and spirits of all types, he was an acutely sensitive man who maintained emotional equilibrium by repeating certain fantasies about the salvation that women provide men.

jimoto 地元

This term for "locale" has a special importance in my theory of modernity. As modern consciousness developed, locale came to be replaced by location, and place came to be replaced by space—everything transitioning from concrete to abstract. In an increasingly mobile world, identity became less "thing-oriented" and more "idea-oriented." For example, increased travel and urbanization generated a type of romantic nostalgia for the countryside that became fundamental to the rise of fascism in Japan in the

1920s and 1930s. Often, modernity arises as an ideal form of a lost (fictive) past. Once centered on the comforting-though-now-lost space of one's village, modern people become focused on the self, which is a portable sense of home. It is a concept of you that can travel with you.

Kannon 観音

A main Buddhist deity whose main characteristic is compassion. This god began as the male Avalokiteshvara in India, transformed into the both-male-and-female Guanyin in China, and finally reached its female form as Kannon in Japan. The name derives from how she perceives (*kan* 観) the sound (*on* 音) of the world's suffering. Some statues of Kannon show eleven heads and numerous arms and hands. Upon thinking about the world's suffering, Kannon's head exploded but then grew back as eleven heads with twenty-two eyes that could see even more suffering. In order to attend to that suffering, she was given extra arms and hands by Amida.

Kanō Eitoku (1543–1590)

A painter of the Azuchi-Momoyama period who is known for his colorful, bold folding screens. He was highly sought after, patronized by Oda Nobunaga and Toyotomi Hideyoshi.

kata 型, 形

Kata means form. Kata is the correct way to do something. In a world of constant change, or evanescence, the chaotic and possibly meaningless flow of existence is given shape and significance by an insistence on propriety and exactness in all matters. In other words, evanescence and form exist in a mutually balancing relationship. As taught in the martial arts, only by mastering the basic forms will one eventually be able to become the fluidly moving master. For instance, as a child learns to say simple prayers, he or she eventually comes to live in a state of constant prayer, where one's very awareness aligns with the mind of God.

Kikkōman

Kikkōman is a major brand of soy sauce, or *shōyu* 醤油. This thin, dark-colored sauce provides the basic salty flavoring that is so common in Japan and in many other parts of the Far East.

kōgo kizoku 高悟帰俗

Bashō taught the need to both rise up to enlightenment (*kōgo*), and to return to the vulgar world (*kizoku*). In other words, the reason to aspire for higher things is to know how to live well in the day-to-day world. One would not want to become holy or artistic if it led to a separation from or an inability to deal with everyday reality.

Kusama Yayoi (1929–)

A contemporary painter, said by some to be the most influential artist now at work in Japan and, debatably, in the world. She worked for a period in New York City but now lives in an asylum in Japan, where she admits to her insanity. Her manic vision of reality is expressed by her long-standing use of polka dots, which for her are an attempt to return to an animistic view of the power of things. Her popular installations of light and mirrors can be found around the world.

Kyushu

The southernmost island of the Japanese archipelago. The other three main islands are, from north to south, Hokkaido, Honshu, and Shikoku. Some would also include tropical Okinawa, farther south, as a (colonized) part of Japan, though this island has its own distinct culture and language. It is generally warm in Kyushu, where it snows only occasionally. Its largest cities include Fukuoka (Hakata), Nagasaki, Kumamoto, and Kagoshima. My family comes from a small village in the mountains east of Fukuoka.

Mahayana

Mahayana means the greater (*maha*) vehicle or boat (*yana*), in comparison to the lesser vehicle, Hinayana, a derogatory term that is now rarely used. Mahayana Buddhism moved north and became dominant in China, Korea, and Japan. By contrast, Theravadan Buddhism stayed south and became dominant in places like Tibet, Sri Lanka, Myanmar, and Thailand. Mahayana emphasizes the notion that all people possess Buddha nature and can therefore become enlightened. The parallel with the Latter-day Saint doctrine of eternal progression is interesting to consider.

Matsuo Bashō (1644–1694)

Bashō is acknowledged to be the great master of haiku poetry, a short seventeen-syllable, seasonally oriented poetic form that uses simple language and avoids interpretation in order to gain universal resonance. Bashō's most famous verse is "An ancient pond / a frog jumps / the sound of water." His disciples wrote down some of his teachings, including injunctions such as "Be bamboo if you want to write about bamboo" and "Rise up to enlightenment, then return to the vulgar."

nomi shirami	fleas and lice—
uma no pari suru	a horse urinates
makura moto	next to my pillow

mono もの, 物, 者

Mono means "thing." Animism is the belief that all things (*mono*) have an anima, or spirit. The term *mono* is both singular and multiple, both animate and inanimate, both male and female. The consequences of this ambiguity are far-reaching and profound. A reverence for the concrete, visible, and approachable divinity of things manifests itself in, for example, the care with which food, clothing, and shelter are handled. This sensitivity to our material reality tends to undercut the conceptual, symbolic speculation that thrives in monotheistic and, by extension, rational systems of belief and knowledge.

mono no aware もののの哀れ

Literally, "the sadness of all things." Motoori Norinaga located the sentiment of *aware*, or poignant empathy, in *The Tale of Genji*. He found it in Japanese culture, generally. Life is sorrowful, a consequence of another fact of life: that all things are constantly changing. Most poetry in Japan is written in the fall, at a time of obvious sadness, when the vigor of summer moves dramatically and colorfully toward the stillness of winter.

Motoori Norinaga (1730–1801)

Norinaga was an eighteenth-century thinker who identified himself as a nativist, or *kokugaku* scholar. *Kokugaku* literally means "learning about our country." Norinaga pushed back against Japan's reliance on the continent, that is, on China and Korea, for its high culture. Did Japan not have its own culture to study? His pursuit of this question led him to a study of Heian-period classics such as *The Tale of Genji* and to a careful analysis of the even older *Kojiki* (712), one of the earliest historical texts to be written in Japanese. Searching for a Japanese essence, Norinaga composed a poem which became inspiration for future nationalists who emerged centuries later.

Yamato kogoro wo	Should anyone ask
Hito towaba	about the soul of Japan
Shikishima no	It is the fragrance of
Asahi ni niou	mountain cherry blossoms
Yamazakurabana	in the morning sun

musubi 結び

A connection, a tying of things together. As represented by a woven cord in the anime *Your Name*, by Shinkai Makoto, it is a fated finding of "the one." By extension, it is also that which brings anyone into a meaningful relationship with someone else: family ties, friendship ties, political ties, and so on.

Nagarjuna (ca. 150–ca. 250 CE)

Nagarjuna was a foundational Buddhist thinker whose writings on nothingness are fundamental to what became the Mahayana tradition. He is known for the thoroughness with which he used logic and doubt to illuminate the limitations of human cognition. His remarkable intelligence had an unwavering spiritual purpose: to help people escape the bonds of self-concern and to embrace the nothingness that would help them see their true connection to all things. The purpose of clear, logical thinking was to gain compassion.

nappa

Chinese cabbage. A mainstay of the vegetable world in the Far East. Heads of *nappa* are long and soft rather than round and hard like Western cabbage.

Nihongo 日本語

The Japanese (*Nihon*) language (*go*). Today, what counts for Japanese is a standardized version of the dialect spoken in the Tokyo area. Because of mass media, this standardized Japanese is understood in most parts of the country. But even today numerous dialects are still spoken, rendering classroom Japanese limited in its usefulness.

Ninomiya Kinjirō (1787–1856)

This historical figure is also known as Ninomiya Sontoku. He was a leading agronomist during the Tokugawa period. An iconic statue of Ninomiya, which shows him as a youth carrying a load of firewood on his back while reading a book, was often found in front of schools during the twentieth century. My parents kept a miniature copy of this statue in our home as an encouragement to use our time wisely and to work hard at both physical and mental activities.

Nisei 二世

Second-generation Japanese immigrants; that is, Japanese who were born in the United States of parents born in Japan. Along with their Issei parents, the Nisei were imprisoned during World War II even though they were US citizens and innocent of the disloyal acts that they were blamed for.

Nishitani Keiji (1900–1990)

Nishitani was a philosopher of the Kyoto School, a group of Japanese scholars who attempted to synthesize Western and Eastern philosophy. He was critical of René Descartes's positing of the cogito (the critical mind) as fundamental to existence. Nishitani held that the centrality of the human self led to nihilism in the West. If anything, Descartes was not thorough enough in his doubt.

Even the self—especially the self?—is contingent on many other things. As a proponent of Zen Buddhism, Nishitani encouraged a thorough doubting of the distinctions that we normally give to things, including the seeing subject as opposed to its seen object. We understand reality when we embrace that which is connected and can be fully shared: the pure intelligence that is nothingness.

Noh theater

Noh is a medieval dramatic form that combines music, dance, singing, and chanting. Patronized by the samurai class, these elegant plays often revisit traumatic events in the attempt to make peace with a wrong that has happened. Often, the dead appear on stage, first in a disguised form and later in their actual state as (often vengeful) visitors from the other world. In tone, the plays are meditative at first, building toward a frenzied climax. For the samurai who made their living by the sword, the plays probably had a therapeutic effect. In these plays, the trauma of killing and dying is met with forgiveness and salvation.

No-mind or *mushin* 無心

A state of selflessness and openness. Zen Buddhists emphasize no-mind as a necessary precondition for attaining enlightenment. Emptying the mind has to happen if we are to learn and become enlightened. Why? Simply because if the mind is full, whether with foolish delusions or with eternal truths, then something else cannot enter in. Learning cannot happen in a mind that is full.

Nothingness or *mu* 無

Nothingness is a difficult concept to understand if we associate it with lack, as we usually do when thinking about nihilism. In fact, nothingness is a fullness. It is lacking only in the sense that there are no barriers to its being shared. Nothingness is like the air in a room, or the intelligence that allows people to understand each other. What Latter-day Saints call "the Spirit" approximates this shared consciousness.

Oda Nobunaga (1534–1582)

The first of the three great hegemons of early-modern Japan. As a youth, he was erratic in his behavior. As an adult, he was famous for brutally suppressing his competitors. He began a military campaign that led to the unification of a majority of the fiefdoms throughout the archipelago. As the most powerful man in all of Japan, he was betrayed by his generals and forced to commit suicide.

okonomiyaki

Literally, all the things you like (*konomi*) fried up (*yaki*) in a single pancake. Typically, squid and small strips of bacon are mixed in a batter with cabbage and scallions. The pancakes are cooked on a well-oiled skillet.

on 恩

When someone does something for you, the expectation is that you reciprocate. You return the favor. You wear an *on*. For example, when the elders quorum shows up to help you move, you prepare pizza for them and send thank-you notes afterwards. When somebody else needs your help, you provide it.

otoshidama

A gift given to children at New Year's by family members. Originally, small rice cakes called *toshidama* were given. Today, most gifts are of money placed in colorful envelopes.

Pure Land Buddhism 浄土仏教

Along with Zen, Pure Land Buddhism (*Jōdo bukkyō*) is one of the two most influential schools of Mahayana Buddhism in Japan. These two schools are similar in their emphasis on practice rather than on study. The single most important practice is saying the holy name of Amida. The Pure Land is an enlightened world in which Amida dwells and to which other enlightened beings are drawn.

Saigyō (1118–1190)

Saigyō was one of the most important poets in Heian Japan. He was born into a noble family in Kyoto but became a Buddhist monk at the age of twenty-two. He lived in solitude for much of his life but also took long trips into the countryside. These later became an inspiration for Matsuo Bashō's journeys. The name Saigyō means "traveling West" and is an allusion to Amida and the Western Paradise. He is known for the tension between his Buddhist detachment and his attachment to nature, as in the following poem.

Kokoro naki	Even a person
Mi ni mo aware	freed from worldly attachment
Wa shirarekeri	would feel the beautiful sadness
Shigi tatsu sawa no	of a snipe's sudden flight
Aki no yūgure	from an autumn marsh at dusk

samsara (Sanskrit)

Literally, "constant change." *Samsara* is a fundamental concept in Buddhist thought. The truth of samsara is that all things are always changing. From this it follows that nothing exists intrinsically—that is, nothing is independent and beyond the influence of other things. All things are said to be, therefore, codependent. A mistaken insistence on permanent essences—for example, the self as an individual, independent being—is a major cause of suffering. One wants certain things to last forever, such as personal happiness. But a mature, enlightened being realizes that change and mutual influence are basic characteristics of existence. If the bad news is that success does not last, the good news is that failure does not last either.

Sansei 三世

Sansei is the term for third-generation Japanese Americans, people whose grandparents immigrated from Japan. These are people of my generation. Most Sansei no longer speak Japanese and know little about Japanese culture, which is often a reason for their sense of alienation as Americans. Generally speaking, we can be better at home in this New World if we have some understanding of who our people were in the Old World.

sensei

A sensei is literally someone born (*sei*) before (*sen*) someone else. Today, the term denotes a teacher or master. In places like Taiwan, the term simply means "mister."

shamisen

A three-stringed instrument used in popular forms of Japanese entertainment. Played with an ivory plectrum, it produces a distinctive percussive sound.

shimenawa しめ縄

A rope with straw tassels and decorative paper designs (*shide*) hanging from it. This assemblage is tied around a sacred object, usually a tree or rock, in order to mark its spiritual power. As a religious marker, it is not symbolic in that it points to something that is visible and present rather than to something that is not visible and not present. (A steeple on a church, for example, points upward to heaven and is symbolic in this way.) The logic of the *shimenawa* suggests that the sacred is not far away but is present and a part of the physical world in which we live. A rare example of a *shimenawa* outside of Japan can be found on Tufts University campus in Medford, Massachusetts.

Siddhartha Gautama (ca. fifth–fourth-century BCE)

The historical Buddha, also called Shakyamuni. Born to an aristocratic line, he gradually learned of a less privileged world beyond the confines of his family's estate. He finally left his comfortable life in order to understand the world better. For a period, he lived a life of strict self-denial. But he came to realize the limits of asceticism and entered a long period of meditation. Seeing that the world is full of suffering, he came to teach a few truths about existence. First, life is suffering. Second, the cause of this suffering is desire. Third, the way to end suffering is to end desire. Fourth, the way to end desire is by gaining a right view of things, followed by right resolve, right speech, right conduct, right livelihood, right effort, right mindfulness, and, finally, coming to what might be called meditative equanimity (*samadhi*).

Sisnaajina (Navajo)

White Shell Mountain. Located in southwestern Colorado, it is a sacred peak that marks the eastern boundary of the traditional Navajo homeland. Otherwise known as Blanca Peak, it rises to a height of 14,350 feet.

Tanizaki Jun'ichirō (1886–1965)

A major modern Japanese writer, famous for his highly expressive sensuality. He wrote a number of carefully crafted short stories such as "A Portrait of Shunkin" and "As I Crossed a Bridge of Dreams." During the War years, he wrote the novel *The Makioka Sisters* (Sasameyuki, 1948), widely recognized as one of the most accomplished works of modern Japanese literature. Although known for the turn toward traditional values that he took halfway through his career, Tanizaki continued to display a modernist appreciation of language as the appealing "stuff" of which literature is made.

teriyaki

A way of frying meat, poultry, and fish in a mixture of soy sauce and sugar (and sometimes vinegar).

umeboshi 梅干し

Salted plums. A common Japanese condiment, usually eaten with white rice.

Western Paradise

A place of peace, enlightenment, and rest to which the Buddhist faithful go upon death. Just as the moon moves from east to west, so are we on a journey to paradise.

wu ji 無極 (Chinese)

Literally, "without (*wu*) extreme (*ji*)." A place of equilibrium, where opposites are brought together in balance. If we imagine the two poles of yin and yang (see image under "yin and yang") swirling continuously around and around, the one being where the other has just been, there is one place that is both yin and yang at the same time. In this diagram it would be that point that is perfectly in the middle of the circle. Perfectly centered, it is all things at the same time: male and female, active and passive, demanding and complying, and so on. *Wu ji* marks the ultimate reality within the ongoing push and pull of polar opposites.

yakisoba 焼きそば

Fried noodles. Like instant rāmen, instant yakisoba—noodles and a packet of flavoring—are also popular. The dish is usually topped with vegetables, but not when prepared by most missionaries.

Yamada Yōji (1931–)

Yamada is the prodigious and popular director of the *It's Tough to Be a Man* (*Otoko wa tsurai yo*, 1965–95) film series, which is the second longest in history. After 1996 and the death of Atsumi Kiyoshi, who played the leading role of Tora-san in these films, Yamada turned to the samurai film genre, directing three well-received works: *Twilight Samurai* (*Tasogare Seibei*, 2002), *The Hidden Blade* (*Kakushi ken: Oni no tsume*, 2004), and *Love and Honor* (*Bushi no ichibun*, 2006). As his tremendous productivity suggests, he had a natural gift for visual narrative.

yin and yang 陰陽

Yin (dark) and *yang* (light) are the two poles of a dualistic scheme of reality as formulated by a major school of ancient Chinese philosophy. Although opposites, each contains a portion of the other, the point being that what might at first seem opposing is actually mutually supportive. Graphically, yin and yang are represented together as two swirls captured in motion, one dark and

one light, with a dot of light in the dark swirl and a dot of dark in the light one.

Thus, the opposites in all things are not exclusive. In fact, one thing depends on its opposite for its very existence. Man/woman, light/dark, dry/wet, and so on.

Zen 禅

Zen is a school of Mahayana Buddhism that emphasizes a concrete, nonlinguistic approach to gaining enlightenment. By bringing the abstract concepts of Buddhist doctrine down into the material, practical world, Zen is the most animistic and, in this way, the most Japanese form of Buddhist practice. By way of various hands-on disciplines called *dō* 道—the tea ceremony (*sadō*), martial arts (*jūdō*), fencing (*kendō*), flower arrangement (*kadō*), and incense judging (*kōdō*)—one can gain spiritual insight. I make the point that in its broadest outlines, Latter-day Saint culture is similarly oriented away from theology and toward material practice—baking, basketball, helping people move, and so on.

About the Author

CHARLES SHIRŌ INOUYE IS MARRIED TO REI OKAMOTO AND IS the proud father of Mie, Leif, Kan, Hank, and Rudee Inouye. He is professor of Japanese Literature and Visual Culture at Tufts University. Winner of the Lillian and Joseph Leibner Award for Excellence in Teaching and Advising, he researches issues of figurality and modern consciousness, animism, lyricism, and monstrosity. He is author of *Japanese Gothic Tales by Izumi Kyōka* (University of Hawaii Press, 1996), *The Similitude of Blossoms—A Critical Biography of Izumi Kyōka, Japanese Playwright and Novelist* (Harvard University Press, 1998), *In Light of Shadows: More Gothic Tales by Izumi Kyōka* (University of Hawaii Press, 2004), *Evanescence and Form: An Introduction to Japanese Culture* (Palgrave Press, 2008), and *The End of the World, Plan B* (Greg Kofford Books, 2016). He enjoys serving as compassionate service leader in the Arlington Ward, Cambridge Massachusetts Stake.